Searching for Bigfoot

Sasquatch, Roswell, the Loch Ness Monster, and Beyond.

The Official Biography of Erik Beckjord: Cryptozoologist

By

M. A. Squire, PhD

M. A. Squire, PhD

Second Edition 2022

Copyright 2017
ISBN: 978-1-7371408-3-2
Squirrel Tracks Press
Searching for Bigfoot

Dedicated to
Arthur Bruce

Acknowledgements

To all the terrific men and women we met in various adventures. We shared some exciting times!

Thank-you to

Danny Perez, liked by Erik, was perceptive and did that scholarly piece of work showing all the sightings and times to suggest a migration pattern visible only after his hard work. Rich Grumley, Erik's sidekick sometimes, was a huge bear of a man himself, about the size of a small Bigfoot and always ready to go "hunting." Dr. Jeff Meldrum lent his scholarly views to the field and Bill Munns worked tirelessly to compare various films and show which generation each film appeared to be, in copies of the Patterson-Gimlin film of 1967. Ryan P. Golembewski worked to bring the 50-year anniversary of the Patterson film to the attention of the public, on the Animal Planet channel. Dr. Bruce Maccabee studied the film with his specialized optical training. To the many rangers, sheriffs, and anonymous callers who called Erik at home begging him to come and see what they saw, and reassure them they weren't crazy. I hope you all kept your jobs and pensions even after we confirmed your findings. To Cat the librarian at the Roswell, New Mexico, UFO museum; and Karen Jaramillo and the Director and the staff there (especially the gift shop staff with their out of this world humor); Tom Benson; plus the memory of dear Jim Moseley of Saucer Smear, lift a glass! Also thank you to all the UFO conference attendees who participated in my research study to compare Believers to Nonbelievers and the general population. This showed that believers in UFO extraterrestrial life were mentally healthy and equivalent to general population measures. A special shout out to Terry Castner of the Willow Creek-China Lake Museum, and the President and her Board of Advisors and other staff who combed boxes of stuff for Bill and Ryan; to the loyal squatchers who were sitting at the Veterans Hall waiting to hear the film was found. Thank-you to Sharpshooter Myron Sawicki, JD, for pointing out the inestimable value of the

Patterson film copies because "Whether or not you believe in Bigfoot, this is a priceless piece of our past culture and has historical value for its uniqueness." Thank-you to Phil Beckjord for bailing Erik out of the Washington State jail when I was laid up with injuries from an accident and lost my job due to not being able to climb to work on the second floor. (At least I hung on in a wheelchair and got my teaching credentials.) God bless Erik's dad for coming up with the bail and getting Erik home. To the radio host who thought we were a perfect foil for each other in our ghost busting attitudes and findings (before the "Ghost Busters" movie and "X files" on TV), I thank you for feeling I was the more rational one on the team.

For my kind true friend, Dennis Marks, who fed me as a graduate student whenever I showed up, my dear remembered producer, director, creative writer at Hanna Barbara, magician etc., who said Erik and I were the models for Scully and Mulder, and Dennis' darling love, F., who both perished with cancer. (And at her funeral her family did not appreciate the quiet man who showed alone nor his importance in her life and his love). And to the only other Skeptic I know who camped out on a Bigfoot campout: Robert Schaeffer. For Panda who is living in my office while I type this on the dining room table, so he can go to school and have somewhere to live; and for my son, Mark, who was a faithful little buddy to Uncle Erik, and who thought every household was this chaotic and he grew up "normal."

And for Erik's honest friend, tool loaner, repair advisor or assister, Art, my precious husband; Mom, Dorothy L. Donofrio, who went with Mark and me to find the hospital where Erik was hidden and get him out and back home, while Art checked with us, rescued animals and kept working to foot the bill; while Mark made sure every animal of Uncle Erik's was rescued and lived absolutely the best and longest life they could.

Now, the above list is from me and what I remembered of Erik's list. He started notes and partial manuscript and from those notes I am obligated not to overlook those who were kind to Erik and who he acknowledged:

Peter Guttilla, author of "The Bigfoot Files" and his following foreword to Erik's autobiographical notes. Danny Perez (repeated, because Erik mentioned you and liked you), Dr. Adrian Rines, Peter Byrne, Bruce Maccabee, PhD, and anyone else with positive regard for Erik.

M. A. Squire, PhD

Foreword

I've known Erik Beckjord for 30 years and there's no doubt he's one of a kind. Gifted with a genius IQ, he's articulate, sometimes painfully blunt, and always intractable in the face of his critics. Challenge him and you'd better know your stuff, otherwise you're likely to feel a sting sharper than the proverbial serpent's tooth. Befriend him and you'll have an invaluable ally who has never wavered from his goal of finding a solution to the mystery of Bigfoot.

Throughout the years, in a subject plagued by internecine squabbling, ineffectual "experts" and an endless parade of weekend adventurers, Erik has held fast to his convictions, sometimes against overwhelming odds that would have trounced a man of lesser grit. When he parted company with the conventionalist camp – as did others at various times, including this writer – the Bigfoot saga had been reading like a dime novel without a plot; the same scenarios year by year, decade by decade with the quarry invariably one step ahead of its pursuers. Over time it seemed apparent to those of us in the trenches that the enigmatic creatures were not merely "elusive," but strangely "ephemeral," compelling us to modify our thinking and tactics. Today, Erik is one of the leading proponents of the "alternative approach" to the quest for Bigfoot.

Whether you agree or disagree with Erik Beckjord, or whether you even care, be aware that he belongs to an exclusive club – he's a "real" researcher and he does "real" research. Add to this a lifetime of dedicated field work, and if the adage "there's no substitute for experience" means anything, it will be to everyone's advantage, casual reader and enthusiast alike, to pay attention to what he has to say.

Peter Guttilla
Author, *The Bigfoot Files*, 2003

M. A. Squire, PhD

Preface

Margaret Mead, the anthropologist, said that now we live as long as we do, we are really naturally meant to have 3 mates over our lives. Fine. I take that. And so, I can with good conscience tell of Erik Beckjord, who proposed the night after Art did and so lost out. He always called me his "ex" to friends after that, I was told, and that they were told to do whatever I said. Erik, thank-you for setting up so much friendly cooperation. It speaks well of you.

When I first was urged by Erik Beckjord to read an autobiography he was working on, though he urged me to read it, I refused. I figured he'd turned into a scandalous tell-all and I was dismayed at being in such a book. After his death, I was going through his papers and found a partial manuscript. It mostly told of some early years and Bigfoot times. His words are included herein and noted.

I was impressed. It was only a partial manuscript and did not include other cryptids or anomalous fields Erik investigated. Erik's own words are included herein and I have noted when it is his voice. He was quite the gentleman. It is left to me to give the final gossip, as little or as much as I wish. God Bless Him!

*

As a byword, I'd like to add that Erik and I were often presumed to be brother and sister. I didn't realize how extremely likely that was until I did genealogy work on family tree...

A young Squirrell female was registered in a household in an official census; dates and disappearances from the subsequent census matched a related family who popped up with an adopted daughter.

Erik's mother matched the branch of that family, dates, and location.

I was informed by more than one person over the years I was the only person who could ever get Erik to listen, and we were always thought to be to be siblings when introduced. One man learned after a while we were not and declared, "but you bicker just like a brother and sister!"

It's also noteworthy how Erik's mother would stare hard at me every time she flew out to see us; I believe she saw the startling resemblance I had to some of her old photos, and how I was the spitting image of my great grandma Lyon-Symes.

Of course, it could just have been pure coincidence, but maybe one day I may just take a DNA test to compare with Erik's one surviving sister…

Molly

Table of Contents

M. A. Squire, PhD

Searching for Bigfoot

M. A. Squire, PhD

Philip, Erik, Ross, Margaret, Peter, Pam, Grandmother
Helen Beckjord

Chapter One
Heritage

Erik's handwriting was small and precise. It showed dependability, persistence/stubbornness (duh!), analytical ability, capital letters shaped simply, with clean lines, the executive style, with integrity and confidence. It raced across the page with no extra curliques or details to delay getting the essence of the letters recorded, as he raced through life from one experience to the next. It looks like shorthand. Most people can't read it at all. People say they can't read my handwriting, so I am getting payback.

In an old photograph of the swearing-in of President Dwight D. Eisenhower, there is a handsome blond youth in a uniform over Eisenhower's shoulder. That is Erik: born Cedric Jon Beckjord, the name on his Air Force Cadet papers. Erik was apparently called Jon by his family. He changed his name to Jon Erik with the Norwegian spelling of his Beckjord heritage. Erik was in

Europe in his early years. He was with his family when his dad was stationed in Germany. Phil's autobiography tells of his love of all things German. Erik spoke some German and spent some time as a volunteer rescuer on ski patrol in the Swiss Alps. He had a huge old pair of skis and was quite adept. After Germany, Erik's dad went to teach at Tulane University in New Orleans where Erik got his Bachelor's degree.

Interestingly, on Erik's mother Margaret MacGillivray's side, his mother's mother was Jesse MacGillivray of the east coast of Canada. One of my ancestors was a Jesse MacGillivray of the same area and time frame who married a male ancestor of mine. Even though Erik's mother was adopted, in those days people had the baby before marriage many times for economic reasons. The wedding would wait. Margaret became the family genealogist for her Beckjord family.

People used to mistake Erik and me for brother and sister. I think it was not just because we looked similar, but because we thought alike in many ways and when we didn't we argued. Erik loved arguing for the sake of arguing. We both loved exercising our brains and winning points. We could each drop it at a draw. We both had healthy egos.

Americans love to acknowledge and celebrate their roots. There are advertisements to check one's DNA to see from which areas of the world one's ancestors came. Erik was a mix of Scot and Viking. He loved the Scottish Games and every year the Southern California games would see him attend. I think I remember him practicing the stone throw. When Erik moved up to Northern California, around 1995 or so, he attended the Pleasanton Games annually. The Pleasanton Games are the biggest and oldest West of the Mississippi. Only Grandfather Mountain Games back East are older and bigger. Erik's MacGillivray necktie was worn enthusiastically.

Erik's mother was a tall Viking-looking woman with regal bearing. She flew out for the Scottish Games one year and went with us. Margaret MacGillivray Beckjord was a tall woman, with gray-blonde hair, steel backbone, and intense studying looks at me, a splendid sight in her Scottish outfit when she went to the Scottish games with us. She enjoyed wearing all her Scottish clothing, and I have her picture taken standing next to a tall and handsome Drill Major from one of the Pipe Bands. Margaret loved that photo. She had flown out to meet me and visit with Erik. It was difficult for me to think of interacting with a potential mother-in-law, remembering my ex-mother-in-law. To my surprise, I liked Erik's mom.

Erik's mom

ENTJ Personality

Erik's personality, based on the Myers-Briggs Personality Inventory, was ENTJ. That's known as the field director, the general, ordering others around and making quick decisions. They do poorly with tedium. They find the ambiguous fascinating and seek clarity. Nothing screams ambiguous like Bigfoot. Implications are that you must be prepared to have the person question everything. When in pursuit of a new idea they can demonstrate tremendous tenacity. An ENTJ is skilled at analysis and can develop models to solve complex problems (Isachsen & Berens, 1988). The way Erik approached the depth of the tracks to calculate weight was one such example.

Erik's father was an army colonel, in charge of all the hospitals in Europe during WWII. Would one leap to point fingers and say "you're not scientific. You can't think!" at an Army leader? Probably not more than once. The thinking can make leaps while the process-oriented person is still focused on separating parts of some fragment. This ability to extrapolate and see overall patterns helped keep Erik safe in the woods. Ideally, he would've partnered with some precise clue gathering personality style. Unfortunately, Erik and I shared the same personality, so we just pressed on.

E= Extrovert
N= Intuitive
T= Thinker
J= Judging

Extroverts need to talk to others to recharge their energy and get a lift. Erik's telephone kept him recharged and connected with people interested in what he felt was worth taking about. He grew bored quickly at a Mensa meeting and would infuse a contrarian view if he felt things were too quiet.

Intuitives tend to look at the whole picture and grasp a concept from the overall view, filling in the data details later. They grasp the forest as a whole and don't focus on trees.

Thinkers can be seen as cold because they don't approach from sensations, feelings, small data. Analysis is enjoyable and natural. Logic and rational data analysis is the preferred method of problem solving.

Judging does not imply rigid negative opinions. It means one who wants closure on a thing; to analyze, come to a decision and act, then to move on to the next issue. When Alexander the Great cut the Gordian Knot he demonstrated this in his personality. This is in opposition to those who savor the process, "P." Process oriented persons love gathering the evidence, always checking to see if there is anything they've omitted. You can see how this could lead to procrastination. To such a person, their actions are methodical and correct. Any person who says "Give me the facts now, let me see the whole picture," "fish or cut bait" "just do it" (the Nike slogan), "make a decision and move on" sounds precipitous or impulsive, maybe unscientific, to a process oriented step-by-step mover.

Erik's Education

After a Bachelor degree, BA with Honors in Sociology at Tulane University, New Orleans, Erik went into the Air Force Academy. Erik said he was groomed for spying on people or someone specific. Erik had favorite sayings or excuses if he was caught at anything. Sometimes he would deny something was as I saw it and he'd utter "deniable." Sometimes he'd say "plausible deniability," or "rebuttable presumption." These sound like they were from his legal training but I think they were from his spy training. He said several such sayings in a row at various times. At the "Spy Museum" in Washington, DC, Mark and I found the expressions listed in the order Erik had them memorized.

When Erik had completed all training, he was called into an office and told he would spy on someone and then kill him. Erik agreed to spy but said he couldn't just murder someone. They pressed him and he said he signed up to serve his country. He would kill other men on the battlefield but not with no provocation. It wasn't honorable.

The man interviewing him said he would not be allowed to just leave after refusing. Erik stuck to his decision but wondered if they would kill him for refusing. He was told they would dismiss him but they would put in the file that Erik was out horseback riding with one of the secretaries. They assured Erik she would back up the story that he was AWOL riding in a field right across the road from the Academy but technically AWOL, off the grounds. He would be court-martialed if he didn't quit. I have wondered if anyone might have wanted to get a hold over Erik's father or ruin him in some way for some slight.

Erik agreed to quit and kept his mouth shut. He always felt he'd better stick to the cover story and give them no reason to look for him.

I believe this is why the President is given the authority to pardon people with no explanation needed. I believe Oliver North was in such a position when he was trying to sell arms to the Contras back in his day. Erik was totally supportive of North. North may have been caught but note that he is accepted by those in military power as a patriot. It's likely North didn't just grab guns on his own and run down to Nicaragua with them to toss around.

Maybe Erik could've gotten away with shooting someone. But North's job was out of the United States . You have to wonder what strings were pulled to bring North back unshot by the local government. There would be risk to Erik's safety and honor any way he went. One thing they couldn't change was that Erik had principles and didn't care what others thought. Erik said "They want to get something on you."

The Democratic Aide Seth Rich's death by shots to the head looks like it might be a similar assignment.

My own dad's death was listed as suicide by the police.

But, I heard the two men arguing with him, the fight to get his gun, and the shot. My sister heard all too, but was too young to remember. I saw the two men dragging Dad by under his arms, with his head all black and hanging down. He was shot from above and behind his left ear, but placed on the ground with the gun in his right hand.

Erik's choice influenced his material success and his welcome into his family, but his conscience was clear.

Erik had a year in Boalt Hall, University of California at Berkeley law school (UCB), under his belt before he decided to switch majors. While at Berkeley, Erik dated Rose Bird for a while (later 25th Chief Justice of California). They finally parted ways amicably. He said he did not want to earn a living as a lawyer. He got his Master of Business Administration, MBA, from U C Berkeley and became a city planner. He was earning a good living and married an appropriate young woman.

To hear Erik describe it, he woke up as if from a fog one morning and said "What am I doing? I don't want to do this the rest of my life." He was bored. One problem with above average intelligence is that you have to use self-control sometimes to stay "in harness" and you have to have some vision of the future to encourage yourself to "stick it out." Erik got his marriage annulled, quit his job, and started being self-sufficient as much as possible to be an adventurer. When I say "adventurer" I am not suggesting a military person for hire. I mean he wanted excitement. Where most men might change jobs OR get a divorce, thinking they were married to the wrong person, Erik impatiently threw it all over to restart with an annulment after a few months of marriage and a new career. His family never forgave him. According to Erik, he was the black sheep after that.

While at Berkeley, Erik made an independent film about the use and misuse of the park called "People's Park" in Berkeley. The film was shown at the Cannes Film Festival in France that year and he had his brief moment of fame. To even have your work shown at the conference, Erik assured me, was an honor. He said it was selected out of hundreds of submissions.

Erik had a busy time in college and graduate school. He was

one of the passengers on "the Magic Bus" that a song was written about. There really was a bus. When we took him to a Woodstock reunion anniversary festival in San Francisco, the players onstage recognized him from the days he was a friend of Ken Kesey and called him backstage.

Chapter Two
Adventure Calls

Erik headed out to check on Bigfoot and mermaids reputed to be in the south seas. Bigfoot took him to the Lummi Indian Reservation. The mermaid quest (you laugh nowadays, but back then it was a hope.) landed him on a shoestring in a canoe in the south seas. Erik paid locals to paddle him around to sites where the mermaids were supposed to be. The locals tried to tell him they were animals.

Erik saw that the manatee or dugong could be mistaken for a mermaid from a distance, because of their overall shape. Sadly, Erik returned home with one mystery solved. He tried to sell his film and information to the National Geographic Society. They would not give him the time of day. Later, National Geographic would finance an expedition that another man would make, to the tune of about $29,000. That man got the credit. Erik's trip was not reported. He could have been published in a smaller publication if he had not set his sights so high.

To fund his adventurer lifestyle, Erik used his extensive electrical knowledge. He worked as a gaffer in the movies, and as a "best boy" another electrician's role in entertainment. Erik combined his electrician's skills with his background in photography and film production. Independently, Erik worked solo or with an occasional helper as "Captain Neon" and his business card proclaimed he was "A Legend in His Own Mind." Erik himself said he was an "internet businessman and photographer who has worked as an urban planner, film cameraman, film producer and director of commercials and documentaries, who has spent 30+ years investigating major mysteries such as Bigfoot, the Loch Ness Monster, Crop Circles, UFOs and psychic photography (ghost images of Nicole Brown Simpson, and others)."

Erik was the filmer/photographer at a minor surgical appointment to remove some imbedded foreign object from one woman who was reputed to be an abductee or wearing a "UFO implant." That film copy material went to the Roswell Museum.

In everyday life, Erik would drive down streets of Southern or Northern California looking at neon signs as they lit for the evening. Every sign with a letter out or damage was noted. The next day he would be out hustling work and presenting Erik's sense of humor showed in his business cards. Erik called on people and got them laughing with him. He enjoyed working with his hands and feeling competent. His ability to hustle and to persuade people, combined with his fearlessness, allowed him to earn a relatively steady income no matter how bad the economy was in any particular year at the various businesses. His skills were hard to come by. Most electricians did not want to work with neon for fear of the gases. Each colored tube has a different gas in it. The heated gases shown in different colors.

Erik's knowledge of all things related to building allowed him to use his electrical knowledge earning a living as a neon sign repairman and electrician. If you drive through a large metropolitan area, it is amazing how many neon signs are partially unlit, or have broken faces. Erik knew an old neon specialist with whom he worked. The man had health issues from working with the different gases over his lifetime. Erik paid the man to do the actual neon bending and working with the gases. Erik did removal and installation. Inhaling the gases is probably not as common with today's OSHA regulations, but it was more of a risk in the earlier days Erik worked in the field and in the mid to late 1980's when we were together.

Erik did not just know how to fix homes. He could repair cars. After a leased Dodge Colt went back damaged, I had no car. I worked and went to school, so Erik looked around for something I could afford. He found an old Ford Falcon, white, driven into the middle of a Malibu field where it sat for a few years. Like I said, Erik was focused and whatever his goal he kept at it. He made a deal for a price I could afford. It was based on a nonrunning car and was about $600, if memory is correct. I paid. Erik got the car to start that day and drove it out of the field. The owner saw Erik take hours to work on it, but discounted all Erik's labor when he saw the car start and wanted considerably more money.

Chapter Three
Erik & Skeptic Societies

"I believe in Bigfoot."
Michael Medved 12:16 pm, May 4, 2016, 870 AM
radio, Southern California

Around late 1984 or early 1985, Erik was invited to give a presentation on bigfoot to the Southern California Skeptics. He was invited to show the copy of the Patterson Bigfoot film which he had. I was present as the Secretary of the Southern California Chapter. presentation at So Cal Skeptics. Skeptics are started as off-shoots of CSICOP (Committee for Scientific Investigation of Claims Of the Paranormal), but legally unrelated. Paul Kurtz, founder of CSICOP and its leader for years, was a true skeptic at heart. He was neutral to all claims and open to hearing or viewing evidence. Most skeptics use the title but it means "My mind is made up. I am not neutral" most of the time. Many skeptics and CSICOP members used to say Kurtz had an "open mind, so open the wind can blow through it." There were many bitter or supercilious skeptics. Some, such as Robert Schaeffer, were truly noncommittal and engaging, not hostile. The head of Bay Area Skeptics, Robert Steiner, CPA, was well liked by many and had charisma, but he had contempt for anyone who believed in anything.

When I moved from the Bay Area to Southern California, I contacted the local Skeptics to hear some interesting and varied topical lectures. Young Al Seckel was chairing the group. He was not a Cal-Tech graduate at the time, but he was a good promoter. The group included Al Hibbs, a scientist at Jet Propulsion Labs, JPL, now deceased; Francis Crick, head of the Griffith Observatory; Richard Feinman, the Nobel Prize winning scientist and a polite and reserved Christian' and a number of scientists of repute. I noted Feinman sat a bit apart from the rest at meetings I attended. He later died of cancer. I became Secretary for the group and incorporated them so they could be non-profit and tax exempt with the IRS. After the incorporation, I was voted off the board.

San Diego Skeptics Chair, Ernie Ernissee, attended some of the meetings at Cal Tech. Ernie was a handsome and good-hearted young man, a veteran who lived with his blind mother and took kind care of her. He was with Elie, a winner of a special international prize (Elie Schnaur sp?), a small, thin, older man.

One lecture at So Cal Skeptics was on Bigfoot. Erik came to it. The Skeptic presenter took the position there was no Bigfoot and all who sought it were fools. At the end, questions were permitted. The Skeptic claimed all Bigfoot prints were enlarged and eroded bear tracks or hoaxes. Erik had brought the whole Patterson Film. The speaker only had a bit of it to show. The speaker had never, to my recollection, been on a Bigfoot expedition. He was what many refer to as "an armchair Skeptic." Let me point out that the giant silverback gorillas in Africa were referred to as a local myth or legend until they were seen by Europeans in the 1930s. All references were said to be distortions of monkey sightings.

Erik also brought bear tracks, but never got to show them to the whole audience next to some Bigfoot track casts he had brought. At the time, Erik owned nine casts, from nine different Bigfoot sightings and expeditions. They would later be displayed in the local Trancas Corners Bar, as the "Bigfoot Museum." My step-dad, R. Frank Donofrio, made lighted display cases for the museum.

I sat and watched Erik's Bigfoot film presentation. It was late 1984 or early 1985. Baxter Hall at Cal Tech in Pasadena was packed. There were the standard arguments presented that the tracks of Bigfoot are eroded bear tracks. Erik never lost his cool. He calmly pulled out various casts of bear tracks and other creatures' casts. He showed how the erosion pattern would look if it was an old eroded print. The shape just wouldn't fit the bear. The bitter hostility and contempt, downright disrespect with which many held him who were arguing shocked me. I'd never seen so many people get downright rude at a Skeptics meeting. I was intrigued. His patience communicated that it did not matter to him what anyone thought. He was comfortable in his own skin. People were so rude and dismissive that I went down to look at the casts. Erik had two Bigfoot casts with him. He had too much evidence. The Skeptics couldn't take it. No one knew how to dismiss literal concrete (plaster) evidence. The speaker would have been smart and courteous to handle them and try to defend his theory that they were eroded bear tracks.

The audience jeered and people were dismissed by Seckel who was furious that Erik had turned up with something outside their normal and they couldn't process it. Seckel said "Get your own hall!" Erik had contributed the whole film to view, which I felt added more to the meeting. He had the casts but was clearly not thanked. I wanted to see them. I asked questions. Anyone who was such an obvious catch-point to the group, drawing rage, anger, and hostility was of interest to me. Remember that "at the bottom of rage is fear." Of what were they afraid? Paul Kurtz, the founder of CSICOP (Committee for Scientific Inquiry of Claims OF the Paranormal) would never have treated a guest or a dissenting opinion that way. He was a gentleman and he had an open mind. He was not threatened by the unusual and was courteous company.

I came to the stage area and asked questions while Erik put things away. He offered to open the case with the bear prints and I looked at them. Obviously, they were of value to him. The casts were in a box with cotton wrapped around them. As I came to know how poor he was, I appreciated more how priceless certain things were to him. Money earned went toward basic bills and went on camping trips or trips to Loch Ness or the UK to search out crop circles. When we would get calls to investigate ghosts and phenomena, the decision to investigate was based on how much gas was in the car and if we had any money to do it. No funds, grants, or bequests helped us.

Erik had a traditional American middle-class upbringing. He was in the Boy Scouts and became an Eagle Scout, of which he was proud. Erik earned about 68 merit badges. Even today, this is recognized as a lot of merit badges. I saw his sash years ago. Even when the Malibu Fire hit, Erik saved the most priceless Bigfoot and Nessie items he had. He did not save his Eagle Scout sash or memorabilia. His work mattered to him. He was not pompous but humbler and more genuine than many suspected.

Chapter Four
Bigfoot Beginnings and the Eagle Scout

Erik had started investigating the Patterson Film himself long before to disprove it. To this day, there is a film called the "Hoax" film. It is in possession of the Willow Creek Cryptozoological Repository. The film was made by Erik to disprove the Patterson Film. Erik traveled up to the Willow Creek area and hired the tallest and biggest local man he could find to put on the best ape suit Erik could rent and stomp around the same area that "Patty" was filmed at. Erik measured the stride of the man, about 6' 6" per Erik's memory, and had him stomp with steps as large as he could spread his feet. Erik noted that the man was about 3 feet short of the spot on the tree where Patty's head had reached. Erik knew he had a mystery on his hands. Erik was the first to call this bigfoot "Patty."

To this day, at least one local in the Willow Creek area apparently insists that he was really Bigfoot in the Patterson film. He is the star of Erik's "Hoax" film.

The Scout Law:

"A Scout is trustworthy, loyal, helpful, friendly, courteous, kind, obedient, cheerful, thrifty, brave, clean, and reverent."

I was a District Training Chair for years in Boy Scouts and also served in various cub scout and boy scout troop positions. I see how the Scout Training went into equipping Beckjord for his adventures. He was the person with whom you wanted to be on the desert island. When I broke my foot in an automobile accident, I didn't have enough medical coverage to fix it surgically, with pins, etc. The foot was shattered all across the middle, over the instep, because I was braking the car for all I was worth when I saw someone was parked in the lane on Pacific Coast Highway. The bones were splintered like broken chicken bones. The orthopedist gave me an aircast, so no pressure would touch the foot. Erik rigged up a rope to the ceiling of the basement and I laid in bed with the weight of the shattered bones helping them fall back into place. The foot healed very close to normal shape.

Erik was an Eagle Scout. He had about 68 merit badges. I saw them once on his old sash before they went up in smoke in the 1993 Malibu fire. The competencies in repairing things and using tools, not to mention survival in the forest, were all an extension of those early scout years.

A Scout is Thrifty & Clean

Erik used his ability to focus on a goal to locate unique places to live that he could afford. Other people didn't use the patience he did and spend the time to see through a rent deal with landowners not even on the market to rent a place out. We spent a few years in Malibu, living up Las Flores Canyon. The nearest neighbor was a mile down the canyon. Erik had searched for a home he could afford and located a property in the canyon owned by a local legend, John Downs. The basement kept flooding in rain and the house was in disrepair. Erik persuaded John to rent to him for an affordable price, considering it was Malibu. In return, Erik put a brick berm all around the home to redirect runoff from the hillside and the basement got a pump. After Erik did numerous repairs to the home, the basement Never Flooded. You could walk out on the patio, over part of the basement, and sit sipping wine and listening to the crash of the waves. What always impressed me was that with all the traffic down below on Pacific Coast Highway, PCH, you never heard the cars, only the waves crashing. Erik rented out the two top bedrooms to roommates and lived in the basement. The basement was a walk-out, level, spacious area. The main floor was level with the front porch at hillside level area, but the rear exit with the patio led out from the kitchen/dining areas, down a flight of stairs to a parking area at the side, and to the doors into the parts of the basement, Erik's studio and work equipment, and the living quarters. The house burned down in the 1993 Malibu Fire. John Downs has replaced it with another structure.

A Scout is Brave

I know that Erik's fearlessness in planning trips to the wilderness alone to hunt "monsters" and the trips to Loch Ness for Nessie searching, and England to hunt down crop circles all demonstrate a strain of fearlessness. To want to search out the unknown and not grow tired of it over a lifetime is rare.

Pets (A Scout is Loyal)

Erik's main companions over his life were his dogs and cats. Sometimes, if money was tight, the dogs would get rice but they never went hungry. Of dogs, he preferred the Labrador. In Malibu, we had a big English sheepdog, Jeepers. He had Jeepers the big sheepdog since the mid 1980's and during the 1993 fire, until at least the mid 1990s.

When it rained, there was a waterfall that came out of the side of the cliff and poured down in a dramatic fashion only observable to us at the house. When weather was dry, you would never suspect there was a beautiful fall there. Wildlife knew of the fall and we saw many deer there when the fall was running. Other wildlife in the canyon included a pack of coyotes.

The big English sheepdog, Jeepers, stuck close to the house. Once, a pack of coyotes just beyond where Erik kept the grass mowed, had their teeth in Jeepers' fur. Erik went out swinging fearlessly and rescued the dog. He did say it was rather "hairy" as he realized he was suddenly surrounded with the dog by a large pack of coyotes. He was outnumbered. He yelled and swung in every direction. I was standing on the patio looking over the scene and seeing the grass bend in numerous places, at least a dozen. I couldn't see the coyotes, but I knew it was a bigger pack than Erik expected. Jeepers was locked in the basement/office after that whenever we left the house.

After Jeepers, Erik had Rudy, a golden lab. Erik had a music box showing a yellow Labrador in a pickup truck. Rudy got run over by a car and Erik carefully packed away Rudy's birth genealogy/lineage papers and replaced him with Toby another golden Labrador.

Erik went for a drive one day with Laurie along the coast north of San Francisco. Many people would drive out to Tamalpais "Mount Tam" for the view.

Toby was off-leash with Erik and a girlfriend on this drive to Mount Tamalpais (Mount Tam). Erik admired the view from a cliff and Toby trotted out next to him Suddenly, water startled Toby and he tumbled over the edge to become wedged in some rocks below. Erik immediately leapt down to save Toby. Erik said it was about 250 feet down and people nearby were screaming at him when they saw him start to rescue the dog. People were telling him to leave his dog, that it was dead. Others were screaming at him that he was risking his own life. Erik ignored all of them, climbed down the cliff and hauled Toby back up. Erik could not leave a helpless living being dependent on him. Erik was bruised and scraped but he rescued Toby and hauled him up. At the vet's, he insisted they save Toby. The dog's back and 3 legs were all broken. After that day, one leg was stiff and Toby tried to scratch himself with it and always missed. Pins were put in Toby and when his back healed the vet said he'd drag his hind end and never walk. Toby walked and could even gambol on the walks that he loved. Toby recovered respectably, enough to walk kind of sidewise, but he was mobile after Erik worked ceaselessly with the dog in therapy with a scooter to get Toby's front legs moving. Then, Erik worked on the back legs. Erik did one-on-one physical therapy with Toby every day. He put an enormous amount of hours into that dog. The dog outlived Erik.

After the accident, Erik didn't let Toby into the house for a very long time. Then, Toby was thrilled to be occasionally let back in, to the other side of the brightly lit living room window from his heated doghouse with the giant cushion. Toby would lie at Erik's feet while Erik sat on the couch by the fireplace and watched TV or read.

The Cat

Johnny Cat was a shy one that loved to sit in the window of Erik's Berkeley duplex. Johnny got hit by a car in Berkeley. Then Erik got Twinky. Twinky was a small black and white animal with white paws who hid in the house. We had to find her often, to pet her. When we picked her up after boarding her once, the owner of the cat spa said at the end of every day she puts all cats back in their cages. She was obviously stressed recalling searches for Twinky and let me know she was found curled up in the tiniest places, where the lady didn't expect an animal to fit. But, when we brought Erik home from the hospital, she leapt up on the bed next to Erik, curled up, and didn't leave his side until long after her dinner was fixed and Erik was asleep. In our house, Twinky favored Art, Erik's friend and man of the house. When we brought Twinky in her carrier on a later visit to see Erik at Brun's House she thought she was going to the vet. When she saw

Erik she leaped up to curl next to him on the bed. Erik had other cats in the past, especially When Erik and I lived in Malibu the indoor cat got outside. We heard a yelp and then silence. Cats are coyote dinner around Southern California canyons.

When Erik and I lived in Malibu the indoor cat got outside. We heard a yelp and then silence. Cats are coyote dinner around Southern California canyons. After that, Erik never got another indoor cat until Erik moved after the Fire.

Laurie Lawrence and Rudy with Santa. Rudy was Erik's favorite dog.

Erik's dad. Erik started out following his dad's path,
Philip Beckjord, an Army Colonel.

Erik in the Air Force Academy:
Conflict between a "Scout is Trustworthy and Obedient"

Erik always had certain sentences that he would use when the occasion suited or when he was dodging something. Plausible Deniability was one of the terms he liked. When I was in Washington, DC, visiting the Spy Museum I saw the ten sayings that Erik used to use all the time. They were the ten phrases the museum said were taught to all spies. When Erik was dying, he confessed what really happened at the Air Force Academy.

Erik had been exemplary in the Academy. When he was near graduation, he was asked to do a deed before he went on to a good promotion. He said he was asked to assassinate someone. He was clearly recognized as trustworthy and had planned to serve his country. He had not planned on being an assassin. "Molly, they do this so they have something on you and own you. I couldn't do it. I swore to serve my country. I wanted to serve my country but I didn't want to be an assassin. The cover story they made up and I had to live with it once I left the Academy." He was obedient to principles, not blindly to men.

The cover story was that Erik was out horseback riding with one of the secretaries. He was galloping along in the field across the street from Academy grounds and so was "caught" AWOL and discharged from the Academy. Maybe his father had made some enemies who wanted to get back at him. His dad was a longtime colonel. I believe this story. I had questioned the other one intermittently when Erik had brought it up over the years. It did not sound right. Erik was using the ten phrases I found at the Spy Museum all his life. I have found this strong desire from other individuals when they know they are near death and we are alone. They want to "clear the slate," "tell the real story," and die knowing someone knows the truth.

One of the phrases was "Deny Everything." You worked your way down the list from there if that didn't work.

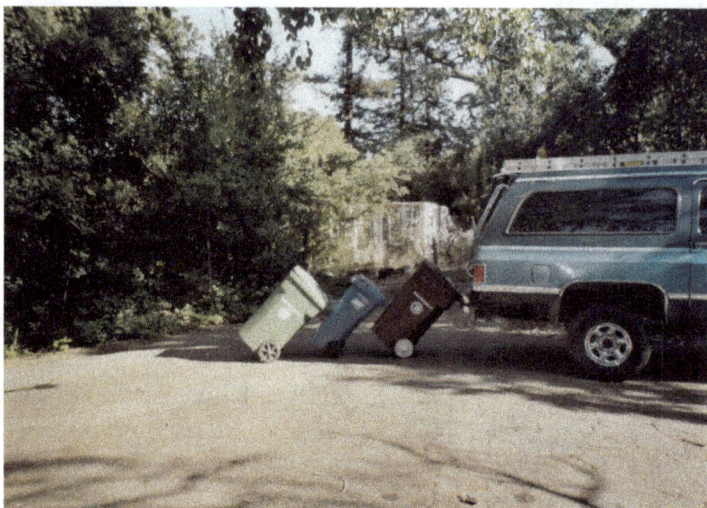

Chapter Five
Scout Values & The Malibu Fire

Erik could repair or jury rig anything. The only person better than him is Art, my husband. Erik didn't have all the tools that Art has, but he knew how to use them. Erik and Art respected each other for their competence. When Erik needed repair advice on the car, Art gave it. When Erik needed to borrow a tool, Art lent it. I could picture them as teenagers under a car hood together because I saw them under the hood together as adults. The part of the scout law that says a scout is thrifty really sank in. The scout background helped Erik repair, make-do, feel comfortable in the woods.

Malibu Fire

Previously, when the 1993 fall (October?) Malibu fire hit, Erik was living up Las Flores Canyon. The track casts from different Bigfoot expeditions (9) were in lighted display boxes made by Frank Donofrio, my stepfather. The whole Bigfoot Museum burnt when Trancas Corner went up in smoke in the fire. What is there now is all new.

Before the fire came over the ridge into Las Flores

Canyon, Erik had loaded a huge aluminum railroad cargo container with all his most precious possessions. He packed it with all that he could find to save. He filled the container with as much of his Bigfoot materials as he could save that would not fit in his old Thunderbird convertible. In the car, to be kept with him, he put as many files as he could, camera equipment, the remaining Bigfoot blood sample from the Lummi Reservation break-in, the Patterson film copy, and no track casts. The Lummi break-in hair had been sent to a laboratory around 1970's.

Jeepers, the big shaggy sheepdog, started barking wildly, Erik said later, as he tried to shove last minute files into his car, he suddenly heard Jeepers' bark change. He thought "Listen to the dog!" He started the car and raced away down the hill. The fire appeared at the top of the canyon. The cooler air from the sea sucked it straight down the canyon. It picked up speed. Erik said Jeepers was barking all the way down like "Hurry!" And Erik was terrified because his car was struggling to run. It was then that he realized it wasn't enough to be in front of the fire. The fire was sucking all the oxygen out of the air. He was struggling to breathe and he realized the engine was trying to run but about to die from lack of air.

Mom and I were in Burbank watching him race the fire. The helicopter reporter had exclaimed in horror "Look! There's a car trying to get down the canyon!" Mom and I recognized it. The TV crew was totally silent, showing one car, one last man out with a huge dog (Jeepers) wildly barking next to him and the wall of flames bearing down on them. Mom and I saw the flames sweep over the house, my furniture gone, what I'd left there. We stared at Erik and the fire. He was Just Ahead of it. We heard the crew in the studio on television sigh with relief as we all saw Erik make it to the bottom.

He was heading downhill to the coast. That's all that saved him, and God's hand. He coasted into the fire fighting staging area in the school yard at the bottom of the canyon, filled with firetrucks and stranded people. His standard photographer's method of getting a feeling of control or removing himself from danger was to take pictures. He took a roll of photos of all the action around him.

After the 1993 fire burnt everything, we (Mom and I) contributed household goods and some neighbors also generously shared. Nothing Erik owned was insured. My front porch was filled up three times with stuff Erik picked up in loads. His spirits rose with each load. People were struck that they had a way to help someone in the Malibu Fire and they were very kind.

Immediately after the fire, Erik lived in a small house or duplex in Marina Del Rey, on a pointed street end across from the Marina. He opened up one room as a UFO-Bigfoot Museum. I think he was there for a couple of years before he went back up to the San Francisco area. He favored San Francisco and northern California over southern California. When I saw Duluth, Minnesota, where he was raised, I saw how similar it was.

Las Flores Canyon and the path the Malibu Fire came through in the 1993 Malibu Fire.

Malibu home pre-Fall 1993 fire. French was one of
Erik's four languages, so the home was "under the sun."

We had our own working fire truck. We thought it would help in a wildfire. It burnt up with everything else in the powerful Malibu Fire. It was powerless against that force.

All hopes were pinned on the water dumping
helicopters. Here's a photo of the bottom of the canyon
where all evacuees and fire fighters mingled at the school.

After the fire, Erik visited friends over time and gathered
3 track casts. He had 3 or 4, until I gathered his belongings
after death and found two. But I know that most if not all of
them were copies from generous friends like John Green and
Grover Krantz, who wanted to do something to help Erik
reconstruct some data after the disaster.

The smell of charred flesh and post-fire ash in the air was overwhelming. One local rabbit tried to outrun the flames

A Scout is Friendly

Many thought of Erik as a curmudgeon. He developed a heightened suspicion of certain bigfoot researchers, but never really developed into a cynic. He genuinely liked people and was known as a genial host of various fun activity groups. Erik enjoyed Mensa and the "SIG"s, Special Interest Groups. In Southern California and in San Francisco he was active in Mensa, hosting "Kulture Vultures" in both areas. This meant he kept track of where and when there would be art show openings or exhibits. There was always a caravan of cars. Erik routed the group through several shows in an evening sometimes. I never knew who was there for the art and who was there for the free wine first.

A Scout is Helpful

Erik met Mrs. Patterson after Roger (of the Patterson Bigfoot fame) was dead. Erik said that he felt she was being unprotected and he made a deal to do the paperwork so she would have a copyright filed on the Patterson Film. In return, she agreed to let him make any copies for himself and use them to study Bigfoot.

A Scout is Loyal

Erik was loyal once you were his friend. Erik remembered what he was told by me of some disloyal action by a former fiancé of mine. Years after I left Erik, a woman in Mensa was at a San Francisco Mensa meeting complaining to Erik of the local chapter Skeptic leader. She said that he let her move in, used her savings, a few thousand, until it was gone, and then threw her out. She was devastated. Since he was a CSICOP member and leader of Bay Area Skeptics Chapter, you can understand this may color my perception of most Skeptics, but I am trying to be fair. But it showed that people's feelings Did Matter to Erik. This woman felt comfortable enough around him to share this insight. And Erik cared enough for my feelings to make sure he reported this to me since he knew how shocked I was when S. broke off our engagement.

(S. tossed me out of the home on which I shared rent and did all the cleaning and main yard work. With nowhere to live in the area, I lost my job in Oakland as I had no base. I drove to my mother and stepfather's in the San Fernando Valley while I sought graduate student housing near my school. He kept all I owned for a few months, while he decided what pieces he would keep. Erik cheered me up and made me glad all S. wound up keeping of mine was my washer and dryer. I have to thank my brother Dean and my brother-in-law Dennis for their loyal work loading my furniture, clothes, etc., when S. let me pick it up.)

A Scout is Reverent

One time on a trip Erik and I drove up to the San Francisco area because Erik wanted to check on how a friend was doing. Marge was an older woman, senior, living in her car, parking in various places outside of san Francisco. We met on a hillside road; she looked a lot like Erik's mother.

When we were shopping for bags of food prior to going to see Marge, I was budget conscious and tried to put in various foods as a mix, dry cereal, canned vegetables, etc. Erik took it out and said "How is Marge going to eat that?" I said cereal by the handful helps and is nourishing if she doesn't buy milk." He said "No. She needs protein more." He didn't want the canned vegetables because he said she could not heat them up. I said I'd heated stuff on a camp stove when I needed to. But Erik wanted to get mostly meat with some fresh vegetables and fresh fruits for a treat. We visited with Marge and she introduced us to her local friends.

We hung around with Marge and her friends.

They suggested to Marge that she invite us to that evening at the church. Marge asked us if we wanted to go to church. We said

"Sure." It turned out that Mother Teresa had flown into town to plead for funds for her mission work. The locals emphasized to us that "She didn't tell the bigwigs. They don't know about this special service. She is to be at (name of the old church in the poor part of town) tonight. This is secret. She said not to tell anyone. This is for all of us." We couldn't believe we were going to see the legendary Mother Teresa. We agreed we wouldn't tell anyone. When we arrived at the church at the time we were told, we saw hoards of people out on the front porch.

We looked and sighed and said "We will never find Marge. She can't have any seats for us." We looked inside and it was PACKED. I didn't know San Francisco had that many poor and homeless in the city. We turned away and went outside and stood there a minute wondering if we would at least try to stand outside in the cold on the chance we could witness this historic event.

One of Marge's friends came running up to us. You're Marge's friends, aren't you?"

"Yes," Erik told him. "She told us to meet her here, but we went in and can't find her and it's packed."

"We've been looking for you. Come with me. We have seats saved for you." He led us through the mob on the outer porch, and down the left center aisle of the church, to a few rows back from the front. We had aisle seats! Marge beamed and we were shocked. Erik and I said "These seats are for the homeless. We aren't homeless."

The man said "No. These two seats are for you" and looked at us with appreciation. Erik and I sat, after assurances that what looked like the last two empty seats to us was indeed where we were urged to sit. The balcony was packed. The main floor was packed. People were standing. And after a brief initial introduction Mother Teresa came walking down the aisle Right Next To Us, slowly and preceded and followed by two of her assistants, dressed in the simple white and blue line trimmed dresses that looked like they were made from linen tablecloths. As I watched her, I wondered as she was coming if she was bad or just had great PR (public relations), or really had Holy Spirit. I was suspicious. I was raised as a fundamentalist Protestant. Catholics were the butt of some family jokes passed down from my grandmother. (Grandpa was raised Catholic in Italy and hundreds of years of art in European Cathedrals was by his Catholic family).

As Mother Teresa passed, it was like she was in a bubble of Holy Spirit and from about 10 feet up the aisle as she came toward me, I felt a rush of peace and love and well-being such as I had never felt before. As she passed inches from me, I knew she was operating with God's Blessing and Spirit. I knew more of God's mercy from that moment. It was very humbling. We had felt honored to have seats saved, and so placed that I could have touched her, as Erik seated me on the aisle. I knew how the people felt when they reached to touch Jesus's garments. They had to be feeling that holy, loving presence enveloping him as I felt the bubble around Mother Teresa approach and pass. I was left with gratitude that I'd been washed in it. Erik felt the same gratitude toward those who'd left these seats for us and the love as Mother Teresa passed. We drove south back to Malibu talking of how serendipitous the visit had been, that his urge to see Marge pressed on him so strongly at that moment in time, and how generous Marge and her friends had been to insist upon saving us any seats, but most unbelievably those seats.

Chapter Six
Erik Speaks

"Will Travel – Speak English, French, some German
and Spanish"
(From one production assistant business card)

Erik has a say here. He had some notes and pages written. They are incorporated into this book. Hear his voice over the years since he passed.

Erik's Remarks:

"This book has been almost written seven times, but in each case some new event, crisis, report, hoax, or photo came up to make me put it aside and investigate or get involved and the book would get shelved. In the meantime, other books started to creep up on me in which my work was either ignored, or simply stolen, including quotes I had initiated. And I began to get an uneasy feeling that if I did not say what needed to be said, having made many discoveries, that others would jump over me and say it for me, with nary a word of credit, true to the backstabbing tradition of Bigfoot research.

The Internet got in the way in 1995. (I helped wire the original Univac computer, covering four rooms, in Washington DC back in 1956, at \$2.00/hr.) the Internet provided a vast wealth of conflicts, advanced backstabbing, and new reports that sucked up my time like a black hole sucks in errant stars. More reasons to delay the book, since there was always one more Bigfoot crisis to be involved in.

Finally, three things happened to push me back to the keyboard and finish the book. One was a major documentation of radical new evidence on what Bigfoot is, done by researcher Brian Smith, the top fieldworker of the new breed of researchers, and the second was the 34th ranked website in the world, Wikipedia.org, which provided a vast amount of frustration by the continual editing and re-editing there of its Bigfoot and Yeti articles. What Wikipedia does is to allow anyone, Charlie Manson, Alfred E. Neuman, the Three Stooges, ten-year-olds, *anyone whatever*, to view and edit and change any article on anything, be it the United Nations or Bigfoot. Then, anyone with information and expertise may revise or revert these bad edits, and in two minutes, Moe or Curly can revert those better edits back to their warped version. Dates can be wrongly inserted, facts deleted or changed.

I entered this mess with many years of information on a personal level and tried to re-edit the Bigfoot, Yeti and Patterson-Gimlin Film pages, and found everything I did would disappear ten minutes later because Charlie or Alfred did not like my changes. My only recourse was to add a link on my website, http://www.beckjord.com/bigfoot (aka http://www.bigfoot.org) to the best past version with my changes, and to my gratification, some other encyclopedia sites also used that version to show their readers. Since my site was number three under the AOL search engine with Wikipedia/bigfoot being number two, this made me feel a bit better. But I could see with no book that I would be the Rodney Dangerfield of Bigfoot research, "No respect." The only solution was to mush on and grind it out. I got one bit of encouragement from a lady staff member at the publisher's offices who said that she wished someone would really write a book about all the fights and backstabbing between researchers. Now, with at least 24 knives in my own back, and many major betrayals, I am very much an expert on that, and it is covered here. For the last six years many people on my lists and discussion boards have kept asking me "where is the book?" Actually, the book is throughout my website, but it is nice to get it in print. Many things left out of the book can be found in the website. (*NOTE by Molly: this is great wishful thinking. It was really not finished.)

Readers who have read other Bigfoot books usually are given a rundown of Bigfoot history, followed by the same old theories and excuses. This book is a history of my own research and escapades. This is not just a rehash of what others have done.

Last, I discovered that thirty years had passed since I started this strange career, and it was just time, especially since I have finally found what appears to be the solution to a problem where thousands of sightings have occurred, and several films and many photos, (many by myself) have been taken yet with no final proof of a zoological Bigfoot. There is no reason to wait any further. The answer is 1,000,000 times more significant for our lives than just finding a mere hairy man in the woods.

Here it is:

The First Inkling of My True Vocation

The Hunt Begins – The Game is Afoot (Bigfoot)

I am told by Lummi Indians that frequency of sightings increased back in 1958. On October 23, 1975, at 7:30 pm, the sergeant (of the police force on an Indian reserve in Washington) was called to a house where something had been heard pounding on the back wall. There was no prowler in sight, but something had apparently torn some plastic that covered a back doorway and there was a broken window. At 2:20 am the same night something was again reported behind the house. When the sergeant arrived, along with several other people, their spotlight quickly picked up what looked like a very large ape standing in the backyard. While someone held the light on, the sergeant walked up to within 35 feet of the animal. It crouched down but made no attempt to run. There they stayed, for many minutes, while the sergeant wondered what to do next. He had a shotgun loaded with buckshot, but he was not sure if the thing was some kind of human. And, if it wasn't, he was not sure how much buckshot it could take. He noted afterward in his report that it was black in color, would stand about seven to eight feet tall and appeared to have no neck. It was covered with short hair, except on the face. He could see no ears. The eyes were small. It appeared to have four teeth larger than the others, two upper and two lower. Its nose was flat. He could see the nostrils. By that time there were seven people there, all of whom could see the thing. But only two others had approached close to it. Then there were noises heard off in the dark on both sides. The man with the spotlight swung it off to the right and called that there was "another one over there." At that point the sergeant decided to return to his patrol car.

In 1975, I was living in San Francisco, working on film crews with NABET, doing tv commercials as a film electrician, grip, and occasionally assistant cameraman. This all stood me in good stead later when I got to work on the Oscar-winning film, "The Deer Hunter" up north. But, in 1975, I was eking out a living and recovering from several frustrating years as a city planner and an urban planning consultant. I lived with my Australian girlfriend, Paula, a sometime model and college student. She looked much like the later supermodel Paula Pozikova. We lived in a quasi-mansion in North Beach, with three floors, a two-car garage, a rear room with a huge fermenting vat for wine, and some grape crushing barrels with machinery, a dog, a backyard, a penthouse bedroom with a view of the Bay, and 2000 bottles of aging muscatel home-brew wine, which came with the house.

We threw many parties and went to many. We were part of the young, hip, swinging singles scene in the 1970's. Yet, something was missing. There was no goal, no mission, outside of becoming a director or a director of photography someday. I had even directed my first commercial, using all NABET intern pals. Many of them went to work later for Francis Ford Coppolla at his Zoetrope studios. I even met Francis. But I knew that for every successful director like Coppola, there were hundreds of hacks and guys on the way down. I know because I heard this while drinking with Michael Douglas at a party, and again on the set of "Freebie and the Bean" when I was an extra, sitting in awe of Walter Matthau and James Caen. I met 55-year-old grips and 58-year-old focus-pullers. This could be me in twenty-five years.

Then one day I was scanning the Chronicle. I read about several Indian cops up in Washington State who were quoted as seeing the creature named "Bigfoot" up close, as they responded to a break-in call on the Lummi Indian Reservation. Not only did they each see it, but they also saw it together. I was hooked. I called up the Tribe. They gave me Sgt. Kenny Cooper's phone number and I talked to both him and his brother, Leland Cooper for about an hour each.

Not only had they seen a sasquatch, or Bigfoot, up close, but this was just one of many occurrences of this type that November on the Lummi Reservation. A Bigfoot sightings flap was in progress. Something told me "Go!"

So, I did go. I borrowed a 16 mm state-of-the-art documentary film camera, sound gear, portable lights, all my camping gear, long johns, and some funds from emergency room doctor Larry Badgeley, a party buddy I met at the Webster St. mansion of ultimate party-giver Arden Van Upp. I hopped a cheap flight to Seattle then to Bellingham. In this northwest section of our most northwest state, Washington, I settled into a fleabag hotel.

I bought a $100 1959 tailfin Cadillac (worth $30,000 today...had it survived). I started meeting Indians, cops, Indians, cops, Indians, and more cops: also, Indian cops and Whatcom County deputy sheriffs. I got a scanner. I interviewed, interviewed, and interviewed. I was everywhere. The plan was to film Bigfoot and provide the newest and best film evidence for the creature. Being a young, brash idiot, I thought that it would be me who would get this, with up-to-date camera gear, while hundreds had failed (except one) in the previous years.

I soon met Kenny Cooper, a tall, Hulk Hogan type of guy, and a Big Man on the Reservation. Kenny and his brother Leland regaled me with their stories of close up and almost close up encounters with Bigfoot, which had been going on for years and years. 1975, for some reason, was a hot year. For the skeptics, it should be noted that the last bear on this reservation, on a peninsula, had been shot twenty years before.

Soon almost every tribal member on the reservation got to know me. I spent night after night on patrol in my car or in the police cars, with film camera poised to shoot and bright lights ready to turn on. As I dug into the stories, and met more witnesses, mostly Indian, I began to notice that things were happening that a giant gorilla would not do. Bigfoot seemed to be weak and smart, rather than strong and stupid. Yes, it could pace cars at 50 mph and look in the window as it ran. But then, they (and there were pairs sometimes) would try to scratch off plastic sheeting from rear doors, and not be able to do it. Then, they could select drying salmon from smokehouses right *after* the smoking process was completed: not before nor halfway.

In any case, they were smarter than I was, with all my bigtime camera gear and superlights. It was as if they knew my plan, and knew my car, and managed to never come out if I was around, or around and prepared. The milkman might see one. The cops might see one, even white man sheriff's deputies. And the drunks on their way home might see Bigfoot at 2:30 am. But the guy who was looking, like the watched pot, didn't luck out, Until I Stopped Looking.

Chapter Seven
Encounter

It happened like this: I had a need for some groceries, and I wanted to replenish some of my "feeding stations" at which I hoped Bigfoot would start eating and returning. It was about 1 pm and I started down one of the long, long empty roads on the reservation. It went through almost undisturbed forest, marked only by a rare single Indian house or trailer. This particular road, Smoke House Road, went down and up, and down and up, over some slight rises. To get to the grocery store at the tip of the reservation, one had to pass by the public dump. I'd heard many stories of Bigfoot contact at this dump. A few times, belligerent Indian youths had challenged me at the dump at night. They wondered what I, a white man, was doing there at 2 am on their reservation. Usually, after some chatting, and passing over a few beers they'd get friendly and tell me more Bigfoot stories. One Indian mother told me of seeing a single Bigfoot "just standing" by the side of the road, that road, on Thanksgiving Day in full daylight, not far from the dump. And she just whizzed on by and did not look back.

So, on this road I was heading for the store. All that was in my head was my grocery list. I was debating the merits of strawberry jam vs. apricot. I approached the rise leading to the dump and I saw a hitch-hiker Well, I often picked up Indian kids hitching home to milk them for info and to get known. I thought I'd pick this one up. He was doing a shuffle, a boogie dressed in black. "An M.I.B?" I thought. Skinny, maybe had a radio? Maybe 6 feet, skinny, shuffling, standing by the side of the road, maybe wearing skin tights…no real sort of a coat…must have a dirty face, all black, maybe a black guy? No long Indian style hair…hmm…no pants, no belt, NO SHIRT! This guy just had fur!

And all my fancy-schmancy camera gear was back at the hotel. I was driving 50 mph and at about 200 feet this skinny guy in fur started to stride across the road. But his walk was a sort of ultra-limber limbo. Arms flopping way up and way back, as he covered the two-lane road in two steps and disappeared into the woods and brush. I got then the strong serious inner feeling that this was not a human walk. It hit me just before the dump: it was Bigfoot!

Being a wiseguy, I figured I'd cut around behind it in my car, and I would "cut him off" and get a good look on the back road. I zoomed onto the side road, splashed through a creek, and found nothing. I went back and stopped, got out and found maybe a heelprint in the grass. There was a game trail. Anyone using the trail could have stooped over, and pretended from a distance that they were a deer, especially all covered in fur or hair. I guessed that was what happened, because I saw the prints on the other side of the road, a similar trail.

I whooped and screamed to the rats at the dump and I was thoroughly hooked. Hooked on Bigfoot! And it was to go on for over twenty years thereafter. Call it beginner's luck. Call it hanging around the dump. It worked. Did I ever pull up the still camera I had cocked and ready on the car seat? Never entered my mind. Like many witnesses, I was too busy looking to think.

I went back to Bellingham, called Paula, and called the doctor. Paula decided it was time to come up and check on my sanity. The doctor did a little dance in the Emergency Room. Things were cooking. We'd all be rich in no time. The Nobel Prize would be ours. We started to plan our acceptance speeches. Little did we know...

Soon Paula did arrive with a friend who was curious about this madness up north. Both ladies came in by taxi to my hotel room at 3 am. For various reasons, I never saw Paula's girlfriend until noon the next day. One does need emotional sustenance for these expeditions and I had not seen Paula for a month.

Floods Hail, Rain, Rain, Rain

With Paula came the great storms from the Pacific, marching in series, one by one, smashing into the northwest Washington coast and Puget Sound. It rained. It hailed. It rained and then it hailed again. After a break of a few days, another would come coasting in. And all this time the creeks and rivers were rising. Nobody had any dry clothes and suddenly the Lummi reservation was surrounded by water. The five-mile section that connected it to land was swamped. I used my $100 Cadillac to ford the flooded road to get to Bellingham to get food. It sort of ploughed ahead like a tractor, dwarfing smaller cars and imports. I got an "in" with the Tribe, because I got the great idea of calling the US Army Corp of Engineers. I suggested that they use some of their stored-away pontoon bridges to replace some washed out bridges. And so traffic was restored. Sometimes the Military Mind is not so bad, if prompted.

With traffic came Bigfoot Investigators: some famous, some not. One who came to stay for a time was famous and a notoriously difficult fellow. I was warned that I might get along with him for a week or two, until he found some reason to put me on his list. So, I made the most of it. A number of times he showed me his copy of the famous Patterson Bigfoot Film. He explained over and over who was a bad guy in this research and what they had done to him, and what he was doing to get revenge. The list was long. II sensed (correctly) that I would soon be on his list.

I began to encounter him and his sidekick, a larger man with a bad back, all over the reservation. Often, they would be carrying pistols in holsters, one holster for a gun, and the other for a camera. Once I saw an M-1 officer's rifle. Usually, I heard them long before I saw them in the backwoods area. I assumed Bigfoot would hear them also and leave. I suggested, to no avail, that guns might kill some little Indian kid by mistake, since each slice of woods was in back of suburban housing tracts built by salmon fishing fees paid to the Tribe by non-Indians. For that reason, and a sense that no gun would ever work, I never carried any. (Note: Erik Never carried a gun. He was a self-proclaimed pacifist. He pulled apart my pistol at home and threw the parts scattered around the canyon by his own admission, after I noticed it missing. Molly)

Dirty Doings At the Tribal Council

Soon the word got out that the Tribe was unhappy at all the non-Indian invaders tromping through their woods, some carrying guns. We were all told to report to the next Council meeting to present our credentials and to request permission to be there and to do research. I arrived to present myself to the Council. I met Kenny Cooper, the cop, and the Famous Investigator. The FI waltzed over to me and said "I've been here before many times. I know all the members of the Council. They all like me. Let Kenny and I speak for you, and we will get you a permit to do research here. Trust me."

Being young and an idiot I trusted.

They went in; the Council members went in (looking at me strangely since I was not going in). I waited and waited. After an hour the Famous Investigator exited, looked at me and smiled, went to his car and left. The Council members walked out and each looked at me in an odd way. They left. I left.

The next week my brother, Ross, came down from Canada in his pickup truck. Ross, I and some hired helpers hauled into the woods, past a swamp, with a gasoline powered water pump to empty out an old well by a ruin of an old house. The rumor was that 20 years back a kid at this house hauled up the rope at the well; and snagged on the bucket was a hideous skull, huge, of a sasquatch (Bigfoot). It was said to look like "a big ape skull."

So, I dug, and dug, and dug. I got down to 15 feet, a scary depth in soft soil. I used buckets to pump out the water that seeped back in. The pump helped me get to the very bottom. I scraped up bones, bones and a skull. It was the family dog, which sadly fell in and never got out. The sun set at 3:30 pm daily. It was cold, cold, cold and wet. As we hauled out the gear, disgusted, we found a police car with flashing red lights waiting for us to haul our pickup truck out of the muck ten times until we made it to the road.

"You can't be here. You have no permit," the Chief of Indian Police told me.

"What?!? (The Famous Investigator) got me one!"

The Chief gave a wry smile and said "No, no he didn't. You never came in to speak and we all wondered if this was an insult to us. You'd better come down to the station and call Sam Cagey, the vice-president of the Council."

Dripping, freezing, and muddy I went. I explained to Sam what the FI had done to me and that the knife was still in my back. Sam snorted and said "Come around and visit me tomorrow."

Next day, I went to Sam's and explained who I was, what I wanted to do, and that I carried no guns. I mentioned science a number of times. Sam arranged then for me to visit each of the dozen Tribal Council members in their homes. This was a good thing, for many of them had made contact with Bigfoot, near their longhouses (religious buildings) and during salmon season. Both types of locations were active during November.

This all taught me a hard lesson early: in Bigfoot work, trust no Investigator and never turn your back on them. There is but one prize and that goes to the first person to bring in a dead Bigfoot body or bones. Investigators will lie, cheat and steal to be that first one. It is similar to the old days of gold mining in California. It hardened my resolve and I was hooked deeper. I learned to look forward for Bigfoot and backwards for Bigfoot Investigators. As Peter Byrne later told me in 1980 over dinner, "God save me from the so-called Bigfoot researcher!"

I found this funny, since at the time he was harboring as an apprentice a fellow who was feeding daily secret info from Byrnes's then-museum display over to the Famous Investigator who was no friend of Byrne.

I did, thinking back, unwittingly get a sort of revenge on the Famous Investigator. Early upon meeting him, prior to the Council meeting, I was hosting FI at my cabin. In between drinking my wine and discussing all his enemies, he asked me if I had any luck so far, had I "seen Bigfoot?"

"Well, yes." I watched his jaw drop to the floor. I

described my sighting (much as I told it here). His entire being sagged with each word. He had never, ever seen one, and still to this day has not. (Note: as of June 2008 - Molly) There I was, a rank beginner, having beginner's luck. He, having paid his dues a thousand times, never had. I hid my pussycat smile.

Chapter Eight
So, What Is This Bigfoot Supposed to Be?

And why are people willing to lie, cheat, steal and back-stab to get to it? For those who are just starting out, let's call it "Bigfoot 101" here. I'll give you a brief primer. This is not supposed to be just another "History of Bigfoot Research" book, (see the works of John Greene for that). But, briefly, the recent history of Bigfoot began in 1958 when a logging road construction crew, run by a fellow named (of course) Crewe, encountered very very large humanoid tracks made at night by something that was curious about their bulldozers. The word got out to the local paper in Willow Creek, California. A journalist called it Bigfoot and the chase was on. So far, Bigfoot has won. Bigfoot creatures (not the horrible term "Bigfeet") are usually over six foot tall, often seven feet, occasionally eight feet and a rarer few nine, ten, and even allegedly twelve feet. The tracks are often ultra-deep, which we will go into later. Sometimes smells are encountered when close to one. They seem often to be covered with hair and look something like a gorilla that is able to walk habitually on two feet, a so-called "erect ape" except that the feet are very similar to human feet, not to the feet of any ape. Hundreds of "Bigfoot hunters" have been scouring the USA and Canada in almost every state except Hawaii, hoping to kill, maim, hack apart, capture, view, study and/or film these elusive creatures. The goal, of course, is Oprah. (Note: she's retired now. Molly)

Apes In Trees, Faces at the Kitchen Window Ten Feet Up

Before my fun and games with the Famous Investigator fellow, I had started when I first arrived to interview Indians all over the reservation. Several described to me a group of three chattering apes, larger than monkeys, that stayed near them as they walked along a road, going from tree to tree to stay near them. Another family described several apes or "large monkeys" on the ground in a glade just beyond a line of trees close to where they were working on a car. In each case whenever the witnesses tried to get closer the apes went away or disappeared. I showed them photos of gibbons, orangutans, gorillas, and various large monkeys. It was chimps that seemed to ring a bell. There were no zoos, research facilities nor circuses nearby to provide these to see.

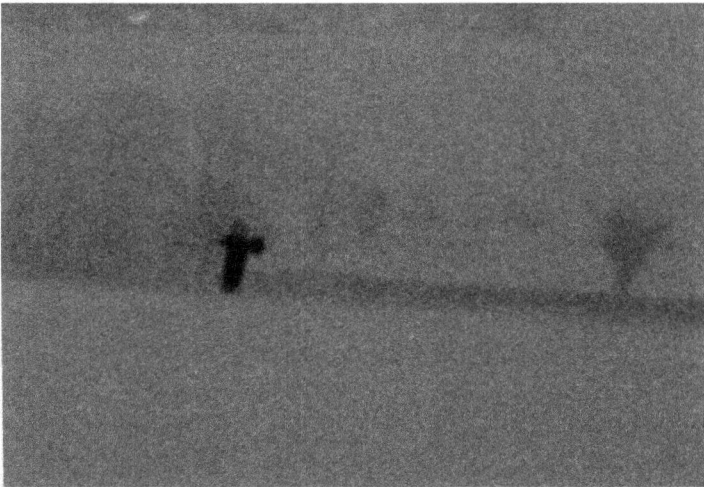

Then other witnesses started to come up, as I got better known. A common theme was a Bigfoot face appearing suddenly to a woman washing dishes, in her kitchen window over the sink, almost face-to-face. One problem was that sometimes the window was ten feet off the ground. The Bigfoot face and shoulders would stay there for maybe half a minute to a minute with no jumping or strain apparent.

Fishermen and the Tribe lived off salmon. They would tell stories of watching big black snags and stumps of trees suddenly "walk off" as they motored their boats by. One famous story involved the Green family (not related to Canadian John Greene). At night, using lanterns to pull in nets, in the shallow Nooksack River side-streams, they would get pulled backwards as a Bigfoot would pull up their net, foot by foot, to pull out salmon. Usually, wen the boat was getting pulled back too closely to the Bigfoot a shotgun would be fired in the air, and the Bigfoot would grunt (aw shucks) and splash off into the darkness.

There were three stories about pick-up trucks getting "paced" by a running Bigfoot that could get up to 50 miles per hour before quitting. One important story came up during the Nooksack flooding. The well-respected assistant manager of the Tribal fish processing plant was out hunting ducks at dusk along a flooded piece of farmland. As he walked along a flooded bank next to a road, he came close to a raised dike that went off at a 90-degree angle. A Bigfoot leaped off it, landed with a splash in the water, ran dripping up to the dry land, and ran away from the hunter, *splosh, splosh, splosh.* Then the Bigfoot angled up the dirt area to cross the road and jumped into another flooded area and escaped.

The assistant manager freaked out, drove to the Tribal headquarters, and was put into the Whatcom County Hospital for mental observation. He did not return from the hospital for a week. He became a nervous wreck and didn't return to work for a month. I learned about this two days after it happened. I found 16-inch narrow humanoid tracks in all the right places. On the dike I found the remains of chewed turnips and carrots. Bigfoot was co-existing with the Indians.

Other stories involved people waking at night to find a family of Bigfoot creatures pulling down the top branches of apple trees to get the unpicked apples. Orchards were popular with Bigfoot.

Swamps were big with Bigfoot, so were quarries. There was one quarry that everybody was afraid to go to alone. Few at all would go there after dark. Many sightings were reported there. I went there several times, alone, at night and felt creepy. Indian friends would not go there at night with me. A few visiting investigators went with me. One day, alone, I hiked in during the day and found "Littlefoot."

Littlefoot

That is, the tracks of Littlefoot. Small, 5-inch, human like tracks sort of meandering around and leading nowhere. I found them in mud. Then the tracks went into the leaves. So, sure, just some Tom Sawyer kid, right? Not. In November nobody, but nobody, went barefoot, man or boy. Few even did it in full summer. These are pick-up truck Indians, in Nikes. Squanto or Tonto did not exist in 1975. There is a television in every house and the yards are full of parts for outboard motors. But, some little elfin "thing" was wandering around the quarry, barefoot and in the dark.

The Cops Know All, See All, Remember All

And on an Indian Reservation this goes triple, because they are usually related to almost everyone. So, naturally, I learned to hang out with the Indian Tribal Police. If something happened on one side of the reservation at six a.m. then the police knew about it before noon. So, with Paula there, acting as a sexy film assistant, I found I was getting more and more invites to go on patrol. One relatively sunny afternoon, we got out film and recording gear into the battered cop car of Leland Cooper, Kenny's little brother. As we were being picked up in Bellingham, five miles from the reservation, Leland got a code 3 call to rush out to see a family that said Bigfoot was yelling right behind their house. Lights and siren going, Leland drove, I filmed and Paula interviewed Leland. High Drama. We careened around corners and ran the wrong side of the road as often as the right. Soon, we came up on the housing complex, akin to a small burb, that had been hacked out of the woods by Tribal salmon money.

There ahead of us was a huge black creature on the road, dragging a kid! I filmed and filmed. We were gonna save that kid and maybe corner Bigfoot. (How do you corner Godzilla?). The car got closer. Bigfoot seemed placid, not concerned. We got closer, closer, and found …a large black horse being led by a ten year old kid. A lesson in delusion. Because nobody expected a horse to be walked in the middle of the road, we all assumed it was Bigfoot. And all over the USA, people were making similar mistakes. A good 80% of all Bigfoot reports are errors of this type.

But, a lot of those other 20% were happening on the Lummi reservation and all around Whatcom County. Non-Indians were seeing Bigfoot as well. I found that I was soon interviewing people off the reservation more and more often. Many of the reports were by fishermen who saw Bigfoot messing with their nets, or just standing on the beach as the boat motored by. A lot of the reports came via the Whatcom County deputy sheriffs. I started passing around cards with my phone number. I soon started getting calls from the deputies at night. Gradually it became clear: Bigfoot was all over the Bellingham/Lummi reservation area. Also, he was all the way up many of the rivers that came down to the Sound from the Cascades.

One Bigfoot? Or many? It soon became clear that no one Bigfoot could get to so many places at the same time and be in different sizes, from Florida to Alaska. Obviously, there are many Bigfoot creatures, mommas, poppas, and babies. One problem: they never seem to die.

With Paula helping, I started to interview just about every Indian on the five by nine-mile reservation. Families would relax when they saw a woman with me. We also had a glass of wine now and then in the one Indian bar in Bellingham. We got into the inner workings of families. Then one family would tell us about the experience of so and so's mother, and the next night we would be over there. Then, the next noon, we'd have lunch with the Jefferson family, get their story, then go to the Greens, then to the Washingtons, and so on. We got to go out on some of the fishing boats, hoping a Bigfoot would show up grabbing salmon. Some of the kids would take us to the dump, where one night we heard far-off weird screeches that did not seem to be an owl. While talking about si-at-ko, or ski-tuk, we started to smell a "wet dog smell." We worked our way through the trash to try to find dead puppies, but the smell would shift and play with us. When we started to put on big half meg candlepower lights, the smell suddenly stopped, like a light being switched off.

All this interviewing got me to finally meet a relative of the Green family. They had several dogs go chasing after something big out in the dark, only to never return and never be found. The father told me about a dark creature that would invade their home and creep along the halls and even open their refrigerator and take meat, even dog food. No matter what locks they used, it could get in. Something big would also go tapping around the house, outside, late, and would tear apart their garbage cans and break car windows.

It seemed as if we had what all Bigfoot researchers want: A Repeater.

I talked the family into spending a few nights with a relative in another town. They gave me the keys and let me use a kid's room, facing the woods to the rear. (All Lummi houses were surrounded by deep, deep woods. Step ten feet back and get lost.) I got all fired up. I, Mr. Big Ideas, would do what nobody else had done. I would film Bigfoot eating my bait-food. I got beef blood from the slaughterhouse, big, big bones with meat on them, hamburger, veggies galore, sweets, fruit, salmon, and even a salt block. I set it all up on a big blue tarp just outside the window. Then I installed two movie lights outside, with switches inside, and a 16mm movie camera on tripod inside, with a Polaroid to boot, on another tripod. The sun went down and it got real (sic) cold, real, real lonely, and very, very dark. For some reason, all the neighbors had left and gone on trips. There was nobody for blocks. Every twig that snapped was Bigfoot. Twice I started and jumped for the lights and found a cat. The night went on, and on and on....and dawn came up.

I did this in three days. By day I slept in my cheap hotel room with Paula and took long, long hot baths. By night, I stayed in the Indian house. One the third night I was dizzy, got dizzier, and in and out of sleep. I was lying on the elevated small bed facing the action window. I noticed that my feet were rising up and my head was falling back. I was rotating backwards. I jumped up and wouldn't let the Out of Body Experience continue. My mind was trying to "disconnect" from the body. I was afraid of that, so I got up and made coffee. I went back, clicked on the lights, and saw a rat in the food. I turned the lights off, set my head down, and poof, it was dawn. No Bigfoot had touched the loose bells and string. The food was untouched. I went back to the hotel and slept 24 hours.

I was awakened by Paula who said Mr. Green was downstairs. I got up, staggered down and he said "Last night when we got home and went to bed, all hell broke loose!" The food was all gone the next morning. There had been yells and screams all night long and banging on the walls. They had no phone. Many Indians did not. So, they could not call me and they were afraid to leave the house to get into the car. Thus proving the Bigfoot hunting principle of indirection - like in Zen. You win by not trying. When you don't care or are not there, things happen. The heavy-handed direct approach does not usually win. Sort of like the "watched pot." Outsiders sometimes have good luck in some places the first night, and less the following nights. Insiders are part of the scene and have other things to do, so they often see and experience more. Some investigators just about have to marry into family to get the same contacts.

There were many other experiences and mishaps. Paula and I got stuck in an icy swamp, and blew out the freeze plugs of the $100 Cadillac in getting out; and we did not know it. The block froze, cracked and the engine was ruined. I sold it for $25. Lummi winters can be brutal. But I figured that the snow would let us find Bigfoot tracks. A non-Indian acquaintance on the reservation lent me a 1962 Chevy, with a driver's side door so bashed in that I had to crawl in from the other side each time. We stayed in a rented double wide trailer home and ventured out between storms to look for tracks and do interviews. It seemed as if the Bigfoot creatures were popping up all over the reservation just a few hours ahead of us. The "flap" was continuing but the money from the doctor was running out. It was time to check on my house in North Beach. So, we did one more adventure where we took a visiting investigator out for a late-night cruise of the cold, dead icy roads around the reservation in the grazing areas, and heard something very big crashing and stomping its way through the thin ice on the fields. Then we had to pack it in and get back to San Francisco, flying out on our last few dollars. But as MacArthur said: We Shall Return.

Chapter Nine
Watched By the Feds, Getting the Patterson Film, and Starting Back Up Again

Getting back to San Francisco, it seemed like another world: hot baths, working cars, a warm bed, and all my friends looking at me as if I were nuts. Someone else was looking at me also: two medium sized guys in suits sitting every day in a green government issue civilian car, trying to read the same newspaper fifteen times a day as they watched my house. There were strange clicks on the phone. Mail would get strangely "delayed." Was Bigfoot a government project? Were we getting too close? Were we an X-File, before the days of the show?

I didn't know, but my landlord had some plans. He wanted to take the $400 a month three story house and convert it to seven condominiums and make a mint. I got my eviction papers. Gentrification had struck. I made a decision to move out and get back to the Lummis while the Bigfoot flap was still going. Time for a change anyway. Meanwhile, I started getting to know more and more people in the Bigfoot Biz and they were more fun than struggling film crew people. I turned in the 16mm Bolex Pro. This one was similar to an Arriflex BL, not the usual Bolex. I gave this to my co-owner, started selling off editing tables, ¾ inch Umatic VCRs I had been selling as a dealer's representative, dumping Sony ½ inch video portapacks (remember them?) and video cameras, some 1" VCRs, all sorts of film editing benches and viewers, and started to move everything to a storage garage in town.

I contacted Mrs. Patterson. I thought she was just being taken advantage of and I helped her copyright the film just in case, even though it had already been shown in public. She signed a one-page agreement that allowed me to have my own copy in return for my help. I eagerly waltzed it down to a film laboratory and then returned the footage. Under the copyright code, I now had "fair use" copies for scientific study of a film that was probably in the

70

public domain anyway, and which had been copyrighted just in case. Then being full of energy, I went to the Mills College Film School and rented time on an optical printer and enlarged every last one of the 951 frames so the Bigfoot in the film was now 6 times larger in the frames. And I stabilized it as well, laboriously adjusting each frame to center it. Patterson had done some jerking around as he filmed, but had actually done fairly well for an amateur. His camera, a Kodak K-100, used a 25mm lens., He had a long wind on the spring, so he did not have to stop and wind over and over. His wide lens got the critter in the frame. The film had been Kodachrome 25, the world's finest grain color film. Not bad for a country cowboy. And I now had the world's best enlargement of it.

I wowed various Bigfooters, including Dr. Grover Krantz of Washington State University, one of the few anthropologists who were curious about Bigfoot; and Warren Thompson, of Redwood City, who published a Bigfoot newsletter, The Bigfoot Biography, and who also went on Bigfoot camping trips with his "Bay Area Group." Thanks to Warren, I made a small side trip with old Tulane University pal Peter Feltus to Vacaville where we interviewed some kids who had seen a nine-foot-tall Bigfoot stripping apricots off trees at night in the orchards. We got some hairs for analysis. These would prove important.

But the Feds were breathing down my neck for some unknown reason. The landlord was threatening legal action to get me to move, and time was a'wastin'. I packed my dog, my Paula (under protest), my camping gear, clothes, and some film equipment in a 1968 Dodge pickup, stored my 1955 Cadillac convertible and matching 1955 Cadillac hearse (white, black leather top), spent a last night out in the avenues with my crazy artist-instructor friend (San Francisco Art Institute) John Basso, and started up north towards Redding, Mount Shasta, and Oregon. As we left, my Tamalpais Film Society buddy Marge Salin pushed a basket lunch on us. We took off. Somehow, the Feds were left watching the Taylor Street house.

The Trip North - This Time by Land

Paula and I, with dog, headed up the freeway pulling a rented trailer full of gear. Being a Taurus, I had that symbol in white covering the hood of the pickup so any Fed helicopter could have tracked us easily. But the skies stayed friendly. We drove maybe 300-400 miles a day. Since we had no real money to speak of this time, just the proceeds of various garage sales and film equipment sell-offs, we camped each night. It was simple. We pulled up into a farmer's field, got behind a hedge, put down a tarp, laid out a double sleeping bag, and pulled another tarp over us. The further north we got, the more often we had to crack hoarfrost from the tarps when we woke.

Bigfoot soon entered the scene, even as we drove north. North of Redding, we woke to hear a big commotion down in a gully full of brush. Using the ½ mag spotlight I discovered deer! Deer travel at night and make noise. Then, driving the next day, some mishaps occurred. Coming down from one of the last of a series of mountain passes in Oregon, the rear brake drum was actually eaten away and fell into pieces at the first rest stop. The rear wheel almost burst into flames. A junkyard trip saved the day. As we went, people were seen less and less and a more pure and simple landscape began. Finally, we got to Tacoma, Washington, and having heard about a suburb named Puyallup from John Green, We drove into that at dusk. It was a mixture of houses on lots, mixed in with deep, deep woods. Many lots and cul-de-sacs were as yet unbuilt. We pulled into one lot and did our usual camping number. This time there was a welcome. About three a.m, we heard a whistle, Then from 100 feet away, another whistle. Then another back, then another in response. There were no lights, no cars, no poachers. Gradually the whistling passed on and went beyond hearing range. All the sounds had come from the brush, not the road. Had we been welcomed by a pair of foraging sasquatches? Might be…

The last part of the voyage was a snap, and we got past

Seattle and up to Bellingham in one day. We coasted into the Lummi reservation with about 50 cents in my jeans and 1/10 a tank of gas. Truly out on the proverbial limb.

And this was all due to Tom Luddy. Tom was the film curator of the Pacific Film Archive (PFA) in Berkeley. He later became a big-time feature film producer. We met because he liked my 1966 film on People's Park in Berkeley (big riot scenes) called PARK RAPE. My film had received a Certificate of Honor at the Cannes Film Festival and had been played there. The PFA had bought a copy and kept it in the archives. I had been discussing my 1975 trip with Tom and mulling about what to do. He said, more or less, "Go North, Young Man." He said I probably needed a change and sometimes uprooting is the only way to solve some mysteries, to accomplish real goals, etc. I decided he was right and thus I started up in 1976.

Now I was there. I had an MBA from Berkeley in Urban Land Economics, a BA with honors in sociology from Tulane, one year of University of California Berkeley Law and 50 cents in my pocket. I was in Mensa and had just fumes in my gas tank. Mr. Big Deal. Well, I started to look up all my contacts and found they were glad to see me back. The reason Bigfoot witnesses want investigators to work with them is simply that they want validation by some sort of expert. I had seen a si-at-ko myself so I was now just as crazy as they were. But perhaps I could let the outside world know that they were not really crazy Indians (and crazy white men who saw it). Eventually I wound up on David Letterman, and the film is in the China Flats Museum.

So, people lent me a few bucks until I could get work. A non-Indian dude in his 20's let me use his house for several months, free, since he was going to Spokane for a while. In his fridge were 20 salmon fillets, frozen. I agreed to fix up some electrical problems in his place. I could, since as a film technician I could fix just about anything. (NABET, by the way, allows one to hold or work in multiple categories: Cameraman one day, shooting 35mm hand held as second camera, and Grip, hauling boxes another day. In a year or two I would find myself "Gripping" for Robert Di Nero on "The Deer Hunter." It pays to be versatile.

The first night back, the whole neighborhood was aroused by endless anxiety and barking by all the local dogs, for hours and hours. They were anxious about something that they could not see. This went on for days and days each night. Sleep? Forget it.

I soon got back into my routine of interviewing everyone on the Reservation, right where I left off. I made friends with a lady anthropologist at Whatcom Community College. She tolerated my babble about Bigfoot and told me "Erik, you don't need to be an official scientist to prove this thing. You only have to conduct the research in a scientific manner. And the main thing is to find physical evidence., In the meantime, take notes, notes, notes."

So, I took tons of notes, and haunted the Bellingham library and the College Library, and read all their news files on Bigfoot locally. I started to spout fancy words like "hominid, pongid, anthropoid, *Australopithecus*, and *Gigantopithecus*." I was Mr. Hot Shot Science and it would be Me Me Me who would find a dead Bigfoot or capture one. Hah!

Bigfoot had other plans. He/she/it was hard to catch. They had even been seen in the ½ acre of woods on an urban hilltop next to the college. So I continued my interviewing by day, and cruising the empty fields at night. I flashed my big-time big light all over, cameras and binoculars on the seat beside me. Paula stayed home and did homework for her college courses at WCC. But she did answer the Bigfoot Hotline number I set up for Project Grendel.

All this took money. I heard from my Indian friends that there were jobs during "turnaround" at the local oil refinery. I faked my application down to show less education, and got on at $7 an hour on the 7 a.m. shift. Each morning I'd drive through the icy roads to work in 28-degree weather. I'd take apart dirty tubes and unbolt old pipes that were 48 inches wide with 36 bolts. I would climb the tallest structures, so I could maybe see a "baboon" sitting out in the next field. One worker said he'd seen one once. I hid my interest for a long time. Since I had worked on film crews, I was able to mix in and made a number of friends. Once, Paula drove me to work. Every day after that I was looked at in a new light by the rest of the morning crew. When she drove out of the refinery lot, two trucks nearly smashed into each other, since the drivers were, ah, "distracted." I soon became a sort of "Dr. Laura" for repairing my buddies' bad marriages.

I passed the cold cold hours this way. Gradually, more Bigfoot sightings were being reported. At the same time, what great beast was slouching down from Canada to pound on my door? It was not Bigfoot.

I woke one Saturday morning from dreams about monkeys stealing salmon to find the Famous Investigator steaming and screaming at my front door. His face was red and his breath came in puffs in the cold. "Beckjord, I tell you, you haff my film and I want it back right now, or I will get Kenny Cooper to throw you in the Indian jail!"

"Calm down. Calm down. What film?"

He puffed, getting redder and redder, "You know damn vell what film! The one you stole that belongs to me!" Well, it had occurred to me that this scene might happen, because no one but Mrs. Patterson knew I'd helped her.   So, I said to wait a minute, I'd go get it.

I rummaged for ten minutes in my stuff, letting the intruder steam and steam. Then I pulled out a 100-foot reel of film and handed it to him, all taped up and sealed. "This has been frozen for safekeeping, so let it thaw two days before you try to use it."

The F.I. snorted, fumed, and stomped off, getting into his old Chevy. He screeched out, burning rubber and took off North. I heard in the Bigfoot grapevine that he had "recovered what was his" and that I had groveled before him. I smiled. In two days, I heard a huge explosion come from over the border as he opened the reel can and unspooled an excellent copy of "Donald Duck meets Mickey and Minnie." I smiled my pussycat smile.

I later found that Grover Krantz, PhD, had worse luck. He used the extra Patterson copy I had given him in some lectures and one day, the F.I. showed up on his doorstep, mumbled about

the Famished Bureau of Infomercials group, and Krantz
meekly handed his copy over. He has been kicking himself
ever since.

Chapter Ten
Breakthrough With Blood & Hair; Coyote Dog; UFO Reports

Letters came through to me from other researchers. Some were bitter, others supportive. There I was in the midst of the turmoil, doing almost 100% full time research, in the heart of darkness, the rainforest of the Lummi reservation. What was I going to do that had not been done already in the last 14 years? We had 14 years of failure trying to capture a "mere ape" and the "mere ape" was making a monkey of us all.

I got some consolation from the Indians, some of whom came to me and blessed me and gave me special emblems and personal necklaces to wear. They too wanted a solution, a finding, a discovery. I learned from them that the "Stick Indians" as some called them, had been around as long as the oldest man in the tribe could recall. He recalled that the oldest man he had ever known had also known about the sasquatches, from the oldest man He had ever known, and so on. Stick Indians of the Lummi tribe got that name from being outcasts, larger, and who would throw sticks into an Indian campout to either let them know they were out there, or else as a signal that some fish or game should be left out as food, as a tribute. I found a number of these stories in the 1970s.

Some Indians said that Bigfoot creatures had been around longer than humans had existed. Indeed, there are references to "Giants in the earth, which came unto the daughters of men" and so on, in the Bible. Erik the Red had reported fighting with hair-covered large savages in the New World (probably eastern Canada). But what, I thought, what would settle the problem, scientifically, other than an actual body?

Blood and Hair of the Very Beast

If this were a beast, an animal, a man, a hominid or an ape, we could learn something from the physical evidence of it. But in checking all over, working with dozens of researchers by phone and mail, I learned that nobody had any such evidence! There were no bones. no teeth, no skull, no body. And lacking same, few zoologists or anthropologists would pay the stories any mind; not if they wanted tenure they wouldn't. So, having some hair from the Vacaville incident, I put out the word that I was seeking more and would have it all analyzed by scientists.

Soon, I got hairs from Maryland. A drunken driver of a TR-3 sports car had bumped into a big, tall Bigfoot, and bounced off. It was rumored that the Bigfoot had muttered something about white man's firewater, and stomped off into the brush. It did, however, leave some hairs in a broken headlight. (I thank Bob Chance of Maryland for much of this info.)

Next, I was given some hairs collected from Oregon, off a barbed wire fence. They were left by a creature that left Bigfoot tracks in the snow by the fence. Details were sketchy, but – hey- either they tested for Bigfoot failed. In the file they went. The samples were filling up.

Then, an amazing break: I was led to hairs just three miles from my rented house. Not only were there hairs at this scene, but also BLOOD!

Vince Sarich, PhD, is a very open and unique guy, sort of a rebel. He is best known for his blood analyses of apes, gorillas and man in an effort to find how close each is to man. In the pre-DNA days, he found chimps blood was closest to human. I'd called him and asked his advice regarding any blood that might ever surface. He said "Freeze it! Put it on dry ice and ship it ASAP to me."

The hairs were analyzed. They were found to:

1. Match each other.
2. Were all not any of 82 major North American mammals.
3. Were close to gorilla, but were not gorilla. (I got comparison samples of the great apes from the San Francisco Zoo. Much Thanks.)
4. Were not from humans.
5. Had some features of bear, but not much.

Encouraged, I flew back to Berkeley and conned a

graduate student into making scanning electron microscope photos of them all, scales and cross-sections. Then I shipped more hairs to Dr. Stephen Rosen, also a rebel, at the University of Maryland (anthropology) where he and a colleague separately analyzed them and found that Wyoming researchers were correct. All this is in the now defunct magazine, *Frontiers of Science, April, 1981.* (Note: I remembered the periodical title as "Scientific American" but I can't find it now, though I read the article. Molly)

Bloody Breakthrough

Finally, after persevering and pestering, I got Dr. Sarich to complete his work, (voluntarily donated), in which he used chromography and other techniques beyond me. He typed the blood, as old and dry as it was. I think electrophoresis was also involved. I "popped in" often on him in his lab. This was when I was visiting the Bay Area. Finally, he was done. His finding was that the blood was from a higher primate. This means it could have been from man or an ape. He could not say which.

However, when you consider that the hairs found IN the blood were from an unknown animal, close to gorilla, this means a high probability that the blood was from the same creature. This means that the creature was a higher but unknown primate, but not a man. In other words, a pretty darn close relative of man and of gorillas. Since it has been seen to walk erect, the best bet is that Bigfoot would be a hominid, the same family as man is classified. Famous dead hominids are Peking Man, Neanderthals, Homo erectus, also called Gigantopithecus. Lucy, the famous Australopithecus, and all of these are long dead, by thousands and/or millions of years.

(Note: more blood samples: the blood was turned over to Dr. Jeff Meldrum, in 2015 or so, in the hopes he could use University of Idaho channels to get it analyzed perhaps for DNA with today's techniques. Erik had preserved it from the great 1993 Malibu fire by tossing it in his car and getting it safely away. After all these years, I had hope some analysis could be done now. To date, I am unaware of any analysis done by Dr. Meldrum on the only known

Bigfoot blood sample in the world. Molly)

At this point, I did many jigs, because after almost twenty years of searching nobody had found any physical evidence whatsoever. Nothing that stood up: No bones, no teeth, no skull, no hide. Scientists would never accept that Bigfoot existed without one of those items. At this point in the search, I was still an amateur scientist, an amateur unpaid anthropologist wannabe. I viewed the sasquatches as flesh and blood animals. In my mad, egomaniacal dreams, it would be me, with my analytic ability, my drive, my moxie, etc. that would solve the mystery. I would bring in the final evidence that would establish a new hominid for science. Never mind that it seemed to be an ape that walked erect…and could not die….

So, I did my little jigs of joy, for finally we had the "blood of the beast." Even in the days before DNA was common and long before O.J.Simpson and his trial, blood was felt to be really a serious, serious bit of physical evidence. The hairs were good, very, very good. But, blood, well BLOOD, it outclassed hairs by 1,000 to 1. While I had not found the bones, I had at least made this advancement that no one else had. I felt way, way ahead of the pack. They began to yap at my heels and have never ceased to this day. To some of them, not all of the genuine "Bigfoot Hunters," it was necessary to make sure that others failed, so they could get ahead. I had much to learn.

The Soup Thickens

Well, I'd made a serious life change. I was up in the Northwest with dog, girlfriend, and my base in San Francisco was vacated so the landlord could carve it up into condos. It was time to earn a living in order to stay there and do more research. I'd been freezing my butt (and my hands, feet, and face) off at $7 an hour at the Arco Refinery. Soon the "turnaround" period ended and I was back doing freelance electrical work. We moved into Bellingham, Washington, not far from the Reservation. We were in a two-story old house with zero insulation where the heat (if any) came up from the living room floor built-in heater. Heat came up through a large grate in the bedroom to heat the upper floor. Cold took on a new meaning at the edges of Bellingham Bay.

I needed a job to continue on researching, so I responded to an advertisement by Barry Russell, a go-getter and entrepreneur who had a small empire of storage mini-warehouses and who wanted to get into the mortgage brokerage business. Since I had an MBA in Real Estate and Urban Land Economics, we clicked. He hired me on a draw and I got a company car and my own office. By day I hustled contractors and builders who wanted to lease heavy equipment or to get mortgage financing for suburban housing projects. By night, I continued my Bigfoot investigations. I had to hide the Bigfoot aspect from Russell who did not drink or smoke and who had only one girlfriend in his entire life, whom he married. A devoutly religious man, he was not keen on this crazy Bigfoot stuff. So, I would come in on time, with dark bags under my eyes from the night time interviews and research. I gradually got to know many businessmen in Bellingham. I discreetly took down any information and leads I heard about sasquatches.

At night, I would cast aside my three-piece business suit, jump into boots and jeans, and become "Bigfoot Researcher" firing up my Dodge pickup with wooden camper shell, and Taurus symbol on the hood. I'd go charging back to the Lummi tangle of woods with a 500,000-candlepower light at my side and binoculars around my neck.

Then gradually strange things began to happen. I'd camp out all night on a weekend night in an area where howls had sounded. I'd put out food by the rear of the truck and then doze off. I'd wake and find a crippled, gimpy, skinny dog with weird white eyes diffidently sniffing at the food, looking at me. Then it wouldn't eat the food but would slowly drift off. Was I sure this was 100% average dog? No.

Coyote Dog

A story surfaced about the "coyote-dog," a weird dog-coyote seen on the reservation. I tracked down the man who had the most contact. I learned that this creature was heavy in the chest and had strong forelegs and thin skinny rear legs. It was bigger than the local dogs and it would maul the male dogs to get to the bitches. Curious, I tried to see it at night but failed. Ultimately, an Indian shot it, he said. He buried it but then could not find the burial site.

One night on a tip from a local Indian man, I staked out a cabin and waited for hours. I woke to hear a weird screeching sound that made my hair rise on end. Then it sounded again, but further away. Next morning, Paula and I hiked back into the woods behind the cabin and found big tracks in the leaves, but indistinct, with a long stride between them. This stride petered out into smaller and smaller scuffles and then just ended.

I looked up the Great Snowy Owl at WWU and heard its recorded screech. They sometimes came down to Lummi from Canada. But, the sound was not the same.

Kenny Cooper recounted an incident in which he had recorded a Bigfoot scream on his police recorder. Then, in daylight he walked into the forest from whence the scream came. He found himself paralyzed; standing still, he thinks, for four hours in one spot until the spell was ended. Then he was able to walk back out.

Was this an abduction? Mind manipulation? Later in an event I will describe further in the book this same type of thing happened to me, closer to Seattle. (Note: maybe he didn't get to write it. I did not find notes. Molly)

A Second Bigfoot Sighting

Usually once you see Bigfoot or a UFO, etc., it never happens again. So I thought. As it turned out, Murphy's Law sometimes takes over and makes for surprises. The first rule of Bigfoot hunting under Murphy's Law is that things happen when you least expect it.

Working for Russell as a Mortgage Broker, I was given the use of a company car, and permission to use it for vacation trips on weekends. A nice new Ford Monarch. I'd heard from some cops and others in the Seattle area that the old ghost town of Monte Cristo had some strange activity going on. On a hunch, I drove up there in the summer, along one of the many parallel rivers that come down from the Cascades to the Puget Sound. Monte Cristo was at the end of the road about fifty miles inland, and up about 3000 feet. There were some old mines there with a resort hotel that was barely open in the summer, and a few campsites along the river. As one got closer to Monte Cristo, however, the camping areas ended and it was wild country. On a summer weekend in July, I was driving up along a winding road that crossed the creek that fed the river. I was heading for the ghost town, when I drove around a bend and was able to see the creek bed about 500 feet ahead. It was a creek in summer and a river in the spring. There was a wide expanse of gravel bed to be seen. There was this guy, a big guy, striding away up the creek bed, as if he had heard the car coming. He was dressed in gray and had big shoulders like a football player. Then it clicked: this was not a guy. The walk was funny. A chord of non-recognition hit me: the walk was not a human one!

I got excited and floored the car. The big guy turned up a bank and disappeared. I zoomed across the bridge, thinking I would see him crossing the road, but no deal. I stopped, got out, and searched for tracks in the muck and soft forest floor. I remember seeing skunk cabbage. Then I walked back to the bridge and found no car, no fishing poles, no bait. I had thought it might have been a fly-fisherman. There was no lunch, no sign of anybody. No gray waders or shirt.

I then hiked along the creek and finally found some vague tracks in the gravel but they were more indentations. But, here and there, there were flat rocks that had been overturned, as if someone had been searching for worms or grubs. Thinking back, the gray outfit must have been fur. My camera? Back in the car. When I saw the creature, I had no time to drive and grab it at the same moment. It all lasted maybe ten seconds. But there was sighting number two and now I was really hooked.

Chapter Eleven
The Soup Really Thickens: The Feds;
Bigfoot Blood

While in 1977 I was in Bellingham still freezing, in a house with plastic sheets on the windows, doing extra work as an electrician to pay for my girlfriend Paula's college tuition and making occasional forays into the reservation to more or less "turn the Res upside down" to find Bigfoot, which of course kept popping up after I left. Or else I would hear a rumor that two dudes were looking for me. Being a young egomaniac, I assumed they were reporters out to make me famous. So, one cold afternoon I was inside sipping broth and the doorbell rang – that drab green car again, and two thin guys in suits. They asked me if I was Beckjord. I said "Yes."

They came in. I sat down. They told me I was busted. "Wot? Whuffo?" I said. They mumbled about video piracy and I went with them as their guest to the Whatcom County clink. On the way out I yelled "Paula call that lawyer fella we met."

After a night of playing cards with the other inmates, mostly Black, Chicano, and a few Indians (I was the only "white man" there), my attorney came and we went before a local judge who was related in some way to the federal courts. Before him, it turned out the inquiry was regarding video piracy and I agreed to talk to the Feds only if my attorney was there. I was let out on my Own Recognizance. The two Feds muttered about how I had "finally surfaced."

In a few more days, I met Mutt and Jeff again, with my attorney. It seems they were hot to locate the names of some dudes who were duplicating ¾ inch videos (prior to the days of VHS) and selling truckloads to bored oil rig workers in South East Asia. The Feds figured I was in on it. I had indeed done some trading: things like "Deep Throat" for "The Devil in Miss Jones" and some feature films for other films, as a collector. The Feds wanted me to finger some people they suspected of doing selling to the oil rigs. I was shown in the next few months some surveillance photos. But, I could not identify anyone as a seller.

However a year later I read that a massive bust had nailed the man who had originally provided me with Sony VCRs to sell to retail buyers in San Francisco, in the exciting new days of VTRs and VCRs. They found 35 ¾ U-Matic machines running and duping videos for shipment. There were also two truckloads ready to go overseas…naughty, naughty. But in my case the charges were dropped. It never went to trial. Ever after, enemies have dredged up this stuff in order to somehow besmirch my name and convince people that I am an evil hoaxer that the Feds once busted. Ho hum. Meanwhile, Bigfoot was maybe found dead all the way back in California.

Jackpot! It seems that, on the eve of the fourth anniversary of the death of Roger Patterson, a hungry sasquatch had tried to break into the home of an Indian fisherman, Mr. Jefferson, on Smoke House Road. Since the story had nothing about sex in it, it took longer to get to me. But, finally it did. My contacts, gifts and interviews had paid off. I knew maybe a dozen relatives of this family. I hustled right over. They told me the night had been bitter, bitter cold. They were close to the shores of Bellingham Bay, where the cold frigid wind blew in from Mount Hood. At a very late hour, something very big crashed against their house, then rumbled around in their yard, knocking over nets and fishing poles. The dogs all ran INTO the house and hid under the beds, which they had never done before at any time. For three nights before this incident the family had been terrified by horrible screams from across the road.

The family showed me the damage: a broken window, five feet off the ground of a rear room used to store potatoes and a few canned goods. The glass was broken and most of it had been swept up. They gave me permission to pull out the few pieces left that had blood on them. Stuck in the cracks were also some black hairs that had white tips to them. Was Bigfoot a Silverback gorilla? These hairs were not over two inches long. It seemed clear that the creature had cut its arm or hand trying to get into the room. I recovered about ten more hairs from the floor. I asked the obvious question "Was it a bear?"

They said "The last bear seen on the Res was killed ten years back. And even standing up, a bear would have a tough time with a window sill that tall. The dogs would have chased it as well, and not hidden under the beds."

I danced a little jig on the way to the car and grinned all the way home. I was on my way to make another call to Dr. Vince Sarich, the Blood Man of University of California at Berkeley, anthropology department.

Bigfoot Under Attack at First Ever Scientific Conference

The day dawned sharp and clear. The sun rose up to light up the dormitories at University of British Columbia, Vancouver, BC. The sleeping attendees rested, and I staggered into the shower, dressed and got some coffee downstairs.

Then I assembled my mini-museum of Bigfoot related items: a sealed bookcase and a foldout board covered (wisely) with plastic. I ambled over to the lecture hall. As I walked up the steps, faces fell. Dennis Gates roared up into my face and said "We don't want you here, Beckjord!"

I replied, wiping my face, "Well, Dennis, you and the lead salvager do not constitute a 'we' so I am going in." And I did, got a card table, picked up my paid-for ticket, and set up shop in the lobby. I had on display photos of the world's only Bigfoot blood, microphotos of the best hair samples ever collected, cast jaws of Gigantopithecus Blacki, a candidate for Bigfoot, and a K-100 Kodak 16mm movie camera of the type used by Patterson.

The crowds loved it. I met all sorts of barely known Bigfooters, including an ego-filled Cliff C., wearing a fancy mountainman suit; Dr. Krantz; Ed Kellogg; Dr. Roderick Sprague; the writer Peter Mattisiessen; John Green; Dennis Gates; the Famous Researcher; the late Barbara Wasson; Bob

Gimlin; and many others. As I walked around meeting people and attending lectures, I noted many lectures were by skeptics and folklorists who had degrees. It did not matter what you said, it seemed, as long as you had a Ph.D. After all, this was science! I showed people my 3-ring binder of photos and enlargements from the Patterson Film, some of which showed teeth, just barely.

Soon, I ran into the diminutive and famous Bob Gimlin, who accosted me in a back hallway. He had heard of my theory that there might be a baby on the adult Bigfoot in the film with Roger. He growled at me "NO WAY was there any baby there. I would have seen it! No way, do you hear? NO WAY!" and then he stomped off in a rage. Later, he admitted it was too far away and could see in the film the possible extra Bigfoots. I didn't mind for several anthropologists told me that black on black at 90 feet is hard to make out especially when the front of the critter was mostly not seen. Others said "Sure, why shouldn't a primate carry its kids? Gorillas do; so do chimps and baboons, even humans!"

A low-light of the weekend was an encounter with Mr. Lead-Salvager, the Famous Researcher. In the hallway, after a few hours had gone by, I had shown my extreme enlargements of the head of the Patterson creature to many people. Dr. Halprin would not let me speak or else Mr. Famous was going to go home and withdraw. I found Mr. Famous blocking my path. He huffed and puffed and screamed at me, "Beckjordt, I hear you are showing teeth in the Patterson Film. No way can this be true. You are making it all up!" He seemed to have taken the same attitude as Gimlin started out with.

I started to say "Hey, look here at the photos…" but he cut me off and pushed me hard backwards. I reacted to that automatically by slapping at him, and he dropped back, stumbled and his copy of the Patterson Film dropped out of his jacket and rolled down the hall, with him running after it. There was laughter, and people stepped in to keep us apart. We avoided each other thereafter.

This was Dennis Gates' chance to step in and act as a defender. There were six reporters around us and he stepped forward, cursed me, and did an old Marine trick: he sucked in hard on his cigarette got it glowing and tossed it with a quick motion of his hand into my face, sparks flying. The idea was to start a fight in front of the press and get me thrown out. Fortunately, I had on large glasses and the cigarette bounced off. I stepped back and called out loudly, so the reporters would hear, "No, Dennis! You will not con me into hitting a known cripple!" You see, Dennis was on bad back welfare and disability. Had I hit him, he would immediately have fallen down, screaming in pain, to get me tossed out for attacking a disabled man. I backed off. More people stepped between us. I went off to lunch, ticket in hand. The forces of evil were routed.

After lunch, a new crisis appeared, the infamous Peter Byrne. Byrne, like Krantz, the famous researcher, and John Green, had never seen a Sasquatch. But he was adept at getting funding and publicity. He had formerly been a big game hunter who got interested in the Yeti in Nepal. He had transferred his interest to Oregon, where he had set up a Bigfoot exhibition in a trailer and later in a building. Naturally, many of the others were jealous of him. Mr. Famous particularly hated him. As one police report states, one stalked the other near a Portland MacDonald's, and there was a brief fight in the parking lot. One would assume the taller man won, using Asian fighting tricks. In any case, in the lecture halls, Byrne started appearing, taking notes and avoiding looking at anyone else but the lecturers while two film cameras with lights filmed. This went on for several lectures, with Byrne dodging everyone in the halls. He was interviewed again and again by the movie makers. Gradually, it came out that he had brought them with him, so he could be in a tv documentary: the equivalent in 1978 of what is Discovery Channel today. His enemies were furious! They united and stormed up to Dr. Ames' offices. I entered behind them to hear them demanding that Byrne and his film crew be evicted and ejected forthwith. Green and the Famous Man stood united, one last time. They both told Ames that if Byrne was allowed to stay they would leave and not speak at the conference. After some hours, Ames asked Byrne to have the film crew leave. Byrne agreed, with a smile. He had more than enough footage in the can. He went away and did not reappear.

What if it looked human and had a head of white hair? Credit Schubert & Beckjord, 1979, for this old Bigfoot.

"To Kill or Not To Kill" Debate

I had suggested many times to Dr. Halprin to have the debate topic on killing or not of Bigfoot. I was pleased to find it on the schedule. But I was not on the stage. John Green and Grover Krantz were to debate. I was not well known. I compensated for not being able to bring up points. I met with a debater in my room and coached him on points and Berkeley style. My favorite suggested response was the quote from the General in Viet Nam "We had to destroy the village in order to save it." It did not occur to me that we had zero chance of ever killing one. In those times, we felt we were in control, not Bigfoot.

[note: these are interpreted squiggles of Erik's about points he wanted to discuss] "The conference continued and I gave Rene a spelling book as he left. I held a press conference off campus. The Royal Canadian Mounted Police (RCMP) reported a "threat to me."

Chapter Twelve
Busted in Pullman: Doing Time for Bigfoot

"May God save me from the young men who call
themselves Bigfoot researchers." Peter Byrne

I got the envelope with an Ohio postmark and no return address when I got my mail at the Malibu Post Office. I avoided bumping into Barbara on the way out. I waved hello to Muhammed Ali, who was headed for the celebrity restaurant around the corner. I went in, also, and sat at the bar opening my mail. I listened to Johnny Carson's television sidekick, Ed McMann, guffawing over at one of the tables with his friends. Stars are so thick in Malibu it is hard to avoid them. I was living in a $1200 a month house up on a hillside with two housemates, which enabled me to live in this ritzy area for $400 a month.

I opened the usual bills and then the mystery envelope. It was a Xerox of a letter from one "Mx Fx" who was bragging to someone in Ohio that he owned a house in the Hollywood Hills, that he hung out with rock star Alice Cooper, drove a luxury car, and more. It was truly outrageous. I'd heard a lot about this kid, who lived at home whit his mother in Twinsburgh, Ohio and how he believed he was a rock singer and guitarist. Half the researchers in Ohio gave me the impression they felt he was a liar and hoaxer.

This letter, I felt, deserved to be read by others. I made eight copies and mailed them to every researcher in Ohio I could think of. In time, I got a response from most that said they in turn were passing it on to many others. A sort of "cleansing of the field," they said. Researchers like to expel or expose hoaxers and liars so as to keep some credibility for the work they do.

A month later, it was time to fly up to Pullman, Washington, and attend the 1989 Convention of the International Society of Cryptozoology, (ISC), hosted by Dr. Grover Krantz, who was a prime mover in keeping me out of the ISC. (Molly was laid up with a broken foot and injuries from a car accident and I would be going alone.) Richard Greenwell, the Secretary, who liked to call himself "The Secretariat" agreed with Krantz that I should be kept out of the ISC. Both felt that if I were allowed in, with my radical ideas, that they would lose income from biologists who would not then rejoin if I were a member. The convention was heavily advertised to Bigfoot people, and papers were solicited. The speakers were a mix of PhDs and high school dropouts, including Francis and Paul Freeman of Walla Walla, who had some photos of Bigfoot to show and discuss. I had converted his 35 mm negatives to slides for him. I wanted to give them all back to him. Of course, I was not allowed to speak due to Krantz. However, I wanted to be there to ask serious questions and to debate where it was allowed.

I flew into Seattle, changed planes and flew to the rural Pullman airport. We landed in a field full of amazingly fresh, green, tall grass and flowers. It was May. I took a shuttle into Pullman. I found a motel and settled in. Then I discovered that Rene Dahinden was in the same motel just downstairs. He had a continual open house going and streams of awe-struck young researchers would come and go while Rene held court. Rene was dispensing opinions on all the competing researchers in the field (mostly bad opinions). We passed each other without speaking several times. To his credit, I must admit that he had warned me not to come to Pullman, saying that trouble was waiting for me. Had I known exactly what it was, I would have stayed home.

As was my wont, since my ideas were too far off the main stream to be accepted in regular meetings, I decided to have an "alternative convention" in a hall nearby in the evenings. I and some others of like mind could present our views. One such was Jack Lapseritis, now the author of "The Psychic Sasquatch." I did this in 1978 in Vancouver, and also in 1987, at Edinburgh, Scotland, regarding Nessie at the ISC convention there. I do not like to be shut up. I was part of the Berkeley Free Speech Movement in the 1960s. (note: how far we have come that now Berkeley students are known as fascist and attack free speech if they disagree with it, e.g., conservative speakers invited to the campus. Molly).

I found a large auditorium and made a deal with the superintendent to use it for a fee in the evening of the convention. I started to make up posters to print to hand out. When I visited Paul Freeman at his motel to give him back his photos, I gave some flyers to him to pass out. I also gave some to John Green who was sitting in the coffee shop. Then I started hearing rumors that I might be arrested. This bothered me, so I foolishly started calling the Pullman Police Department to ask about this. I went to the station house several times to find out what was going on. I had no idea what I could be up for, since I had done nothing wrong in Pullman. I naively thought I could stop this before it ever happened by protesting my innocence. Silly Boy. The afternoon before the evening session of the convention started. I went one more time to inquire at the Police Department. Big Mistake. At the desk, they asked for my identification. Then they said "Wait a minute." Six cops came out with guns drawn and handcuffed me. There was a warrant from the county District Attorney, not the city.

Two cops drove me to the county jail, in handcuffs, through those green lush fields of grass. I foolishly started talking about a False Arrest Lawsuit. Of course, they later reported this to the DA's office. I was put in the County Jail and booked, photographed, searched, and fingerprinted like a common criminal. The jailers did give me a Yellow Pages telephone directory to search for an attorney. I used my psychic skills to finally select one. It turned out to be a lady ex-judge. I told her I had found out I was busted on bogus charges of making death threats to Freddie in Ohio, which I had never done. By some twisted legal logic, the Junior Deputy District Attorney, another lady and new to her job, had bought Freddie's story, never asking for his identification. She had decided that even though the letters were allegedly mailed from California to Ohio, since they threatened death to Freddie in Pullman, I could be busted in Pullman. I was charged with coercion and harassment and also given a restraining order to stay away from the convention I had flown there to attend!

As the cell door slammed, I was pretty down and had some dark moments, wondering how this kid could have pulled this off. I called my dad and he arranged with a local bail bondsman to come out the next day to spring me. But, I had to spend one night there, even doing sweeping and mopping the cell block. Later in the evening one of the deputies did me a huge favor and gave me a folder of Xerox copies of the alleged evidence for the death threats. I feverishly looked through them and was amazed to see my own letterhead stationery had been Xeroxed and recreated to write faked letters! There were five threat letters, cussing out Freddie and saying he would be killed in Pullman if he showed up. They were signed by an "Eric Bejordk" – not even my name! At no place was my real name ever typed in, nor signed.

When my attorney came the next day to get me out with the bailbondsman, I showed these to her. We went to the judge who had signed the restraining order at his home. Fortunately, I was wearing a suit and I kept my mouth shut. My attorney showed him the fake letters and explained this was a conflict between nut-case Bigfoot researchers, and the signatures were not even my name. He shook his head and signed a paper allowing me to stay in town, but not to attend the convention, pending a court hearing a week AFTER the events. This blew my mind and I began to learn more about back-country Washington state justice. Faked stationery, false and wrongly spelled signature, no identification for the complainant, and still I was charged. I was flabbergasted, remembering my Boalt Hall law schooling.

I tried to see the DA at his office and left letters explaining this. They would not let me see him. I called at home to the Junior Deputy DA lady and explained all this. She ignored it, saying, "Show it in court." I called the Pullman Herald and they did listen. They interviewed me. The article came out in banner headlines, "BIGFOOT CONVENTION ERUPTS IN DEATH THREATS AND

ARRESTS!" I pushed the theme that my enemies had gotten me busted to prevent my views from being heard. Krantz was heard to growl that the "Beckjord arrest has gotten more news than the convention itself ever could have." The Associated Press picked up the story. The event was printed in hundreds of papers, including the (national newsstand paper). Paradoxically, I managed to get more attention to my theories on Bigfoot by being in jail than I ever could have by attending the convention, where plans were afoot to prevent me from saying anything in public.

The next bad news was that the superintendent called my motel and left word he was cancelling my meeting in the hall to "avoid trouble." Being a jailbird, my money was no good and was refunded. Contrary to American tradition, I was guilty before even going to trial. So, not giving up, I rented a large suite in the same motel where I was staying. I put out new flyers announcing the new location for the alternative conference. I stood on the path leading to the ISC meeting and passed out my flyers. Some people came to shake my hand and others averted their heads and walked past. John Green said some good things on my behalf at the convention, mentioning the letters had been faked. Someone, perhaps Dahinden, had given my real letters to Francis so he could cut off the letterhead and make fake stationery.

My alternative meeting was a success, for about 50% of the people who attended the main meeting also came over to mine, at different times. As often happens, rebels with new info banned at regular meetings many times will have the real hot new information that is just unacceptable to the Old Guard gatekeepers at regular conventions. Many people sense this and seek out the new information. At my meeting, I projected the large version of the Patterson Gimlin Film that I had created on an optical printer at Mills College. I played it over and over in slow motion, forwards and backwards, on a special 16mm analysis projector I brought with me. I also showed slides based on the film that were enlarged 200 times that showed odd things in the film not usually noticed. One success was the Bigfoot Baby seen on the chest of the mother in frame 370. A number of Bigfooters left the room saying "I see it! I see it!" One was Henry May, a graduate student of Krantz's from Washington State University, WSU.

I also showed the series of stills from the 1978-1981 Sierra Ponds Expeditions. These caused great confusion since the beings did not look like what the Bigfooters expected to see, which was more of the Patterson creature. [note: "Lapseritis no show" per note. M]

Then, the day after the convention closed I tried once more to see the DA and was refused. So, I took the shuttle out to the airport and spent time sitting with Dr. Roy Mackal, who was an author on the subject of Nessie and also on the Board of the ISC. We did not discuss the ISC politics, but he did mention he was extremely unimpressed by presentations by Twigger and others and wondered why Krantz had selected them as speakers. I never had time to tell him about the 16mm film I'd taken of Nessie in 1983, when I was at the Loch. Then I flew home, upset but also gratified by the events. For indeed, I now was far better known to the world at large, more so than if I had spoken at the main convention. As Dahinden later said, "You should be thankful. The publicity you got from that was incredible." [Note: Erik had been in phone contact during all this. I was in bed, no car, with my foot in the rope sling he had set up for my broken foot. I couldn't help him during all this crisis.M]

Back at home, I started to fight my legal battle by long distance. Things progressed when I found out from Ohio researchers that "Mark Francis" was really a Freddy Twigger. I was able to get his car and driver's license numbers from Ohio DMV. I hired a handwriting analyst who provided affidavits that my handwriting was never on the fake signatures. My attorney, whom everyone knew and respected in court, being a former judge of that same court, appeared several times with this new evidence, telling the DA to his face that "Your people never checked the identification of the complainant and he filed using a fake name." He blanched at that and hurried off.

Finally, the crucial piece of evidence came to me from Ohio researcher Don Keating. He wrote me and told me that he had driven frm Ohio to Washington in Francis' beat up old car, to save air fare. During the trip, Francis had revealed his entire plot to Keating! That Francis had faked the letters ad was going to show them to cops in Pullman to get me in jail. He also revealed that Francis carried a .32 automatic pistol with him at all times, even in the DA's office! He was ready, he said, to shoot me if I assaulted him at the meeting.

Although I privately wondered why Don did not speak up in Pullman and get me out of jail, I was glad he had at least come forth on it later and he did sign a notarized affidavit which he sent to me. I forwarded it to my attorney. She showed it to the judge and the judge said "This case is amazing. And, the file is already five inches thick. Case dismissed!" [note: Don needed a ride home. I don't think he would've had one with Freddie if he'd squealed. M]

I placed a curse on Freddie boy when I found I was unable to sue him nor the Pullman DA's office after a huge amount of research and long distance calls. In 1998 I was given some photos to download from one of Keating's yearly seminars. There was Freddie, now weighing maybe 300 pounds, looking dazed and lost. His wanna-be-rock and roll career had crashed. Revenge is sweet. Every researcher in the United States knew what he had done. The publicity he had gotten for me was more than $100,000 could have bought. Thanks, Freddie!

Erik on the Dave Letterman Show with his sculpted Bigfoot Head and talking about Bigfoot.

M. A. Squire, PhD

BECKJORD HEAD   LETTERMAN HEAD

BIGFOOT HEAD

UFO, BIGFOOT & LOCH
NESS MONSTER MUSEUM
709 UNION ST.
S.F., CA 94133

Chapter Thirteen
Various Stories: What/Who is Bigfoot

Bigfoot could be a flesh and blood being that has special powers. Some Bigfoots may be dropped off as agents by UFO aliens. There are also stories galore from Indians, collected in the 1920's. they describe a large, strong, secretive humanoid that can successfully breed with humans, steal fish and game from humans, hypnotize humans, and according to some Indian reports go invisible at will. They live in caves hidden by animal skins or brush or even large boulders. They are often at the top of a mountain or in the center of a remote wilderness.

Kidnapped victims who escape tell stories about sleeping under trees, as nomads, sleeping in dirt caves, using fire for heat but not for cooking, living in underground bell-shaped enclosures, living under rock ledges, and living in natural caves, or dug out caves that have a long dirt tunnel to reach them.

One story by "Randy" has large Indians capturing him and taking him to Mt. St. Helens, into an elaborate tunnel system where they lived and held ceremonies. He ultimately escaped and somehow pushed two of his pursuers off a cliff. He was found four days later at his campsite by fellow campers. They reported him as scratched up and exhausted. He did not mention the Indians as Hair Covered.

I spent several years starting in 1975, living on the Lummi Indian reservation, near Bellingham, Washington. I also later lived in Bellingham and Seattle. The area was 3 x 9 miles in size, with half of it open fields and marshes. Basically, I followed up on reports during a "flap" of sightings. I obtained one sighting there myself and another sighting in the nearby Cascades with other sightings to follow later. I also "turned upside down" the reservation lands to locate any Bigfoot sleeping spots, habitual trails, encampments, etc. I found tracks, often solo tracks (only one footprint), and others that led to marshy weeds that did not register impressions. I also found tracks that morphed (in snow) from naked humanoid foot to boot tracks, as described in another chapter, plus tracks that "ended" in snow near Tacoma in a semi-rural area. I found no caves, no beds, no places under cavities in trees, and no heavy-use trails. I hiked back into the most dense and most remote places in the rain forest there, places where no one had ever gone before. Bigfoot was a phantom that appeared, stole apples from trees, knocked on walls, crossed roads when people driving would say "Wouldn't this be a great time for Bigfoot to appear?" And then Bigfoot appeared, as has happened at Loch Ness with the Loch Ness Monster. (note: yes, exactly as I saw it. M)

I was mentally threatened when I played baby screams on a tape. I smelled "wet dog" smell which others smelled, at the garbage dump. The smell ceased once we discussed it. I've heard strange cries and screams in the distance, followed many tracks, and interviewed 175 persons who had made sightings.

What to Make of This?

If Bigfoot creatures are 100% flesh and blood, as large primates, heavy, they will leave trails that do not disappear, just as deer do. If Bigfoot do have such trails, they will lead to a cave, or opening under a large tree, or a den under a tree-fall tangle. There may even be the claimed dug-out downward bell cave. This never was found. No Trace.

See if you can see at least two Bigfoots in this "Pond" photograph.

Bottom is to the left. It is the reflecting pond.

Chapter Fourteen
Patterson-Gimlin Film Analysis;
Bigfoot Trips

Erik had his copies of the Patterson Film, courtesy of friendship and assistance to Mrs. Patterson after Roger Patterson passed. The Films were evaluated by an analyst who made it his contribution to the field to rate each copy he found in the distance he measured by copy imperfections that indicated how close it was to the original film. Whether the imperfections were on the original Patterson film or not is not known. So, this is a certain amount of guesswork.

Bill Munns did the evaluation of films and said he'd donate film copies received from Dr. Jeff Meldrum to the Bigfoot Museum. He saw the film sent to Dr. Bruce Maccabbee, and compared copies. Bill believes the copies he saw at the Willow Creek Museum were from Maccabee's copy.

I heard that the film analysis, frame by frame, revealed callouses and creases as the foot bent in movement. It is hard to hang onto genuine unusual materials. The four hair analyses from four different states did not result in even one hair from any sample being returned. Recognition of the fact that nothing is ever seen again after it leaves your hands led Erik to hold onto some of the bloody broken glass from the Lummi Reservation. I sent it off for analysis. It has not been returned nor has it been analyzed to my knowledge.

Typical Bigfoot Investigations

I defy the average alleged, self-reported Bigfoot Researcher to know the difference between a cat hole and a latrine, let alone when you must choose one over the other and how far you must be from various water sources. With my boy scout leader training, I'm aware of how much more competent in the woods Erik was than the average Joe.

One winter, Erik got a call from the desert outside Lancaster. It'd been snowing. We drove up and tramped around in the snow because someone had reported a Bigfoot sighting. We were lurching around an area of   slightly rolling terrain when we spotted fresh tracks in the snow. The snow had fallen fresh the evening before. The tracks were large boxy footprints, sinking straight down in the snow. They were not melted or distorted.

The two men with us were terribly excited because they followed the tracks to a spot from which you could observe the house of one of them. The house was within 50 yards of the tracks. Erik pooh poohed it and said he drove a long way just for more tracks. The tracks vanished into the hills. This was one of the times we were with Rich Grumley.

One time, we were called to the desert again and there was no snow. The tracks were in dirt. They headed up over a hill or two and kept going to the direction of the Eastern Sierra Mountains.

Another time, we camped around Fish Creek in the Sierras. We hadn't even finished setting up camp when some of us took a break to see any evidence of Bigfoot before it got too dark. One fellow shouted and another with him went running for Erik. They said they thought they were alone until they saw a fellow in the stream. They thought he was fishing. He looked so wide and bulky that they wondered why he was wearing a raincoat. He suddenly was walking "straight up the mountain" and they were left behind marveling at how the man in the dark raincoat could walk straight up the mountain with huge strides and they couldn't even get a toe-hold. They were very excited and said as they tried to keep up with "the man in the raincoat" they realized he wasn't wearing a raincoat.

By the time they'd run back to Erik, the individual was up the mountain and gone from view. I saw about three or four seconds of him. It was like watching a fly walk up a wall. Then the trees hid him from view. The rest of the trip we didn't see any Bigfoot. Fish Camp was kind of Erik's "go to" place when he wanted to go looking and didn't have any current reports to follow.

Reports

In those early days I had a Xerox 850 word processor. That was the extent of the personal computer field, along with the Radio Shack TRS-80. There was no internet, no world-wide web, no emails. People would telephone from around the globe to report unusual occurrences. Much of the income went on huge phone bills, at least $200 a month in the days of no competition and $20 phone service with charges by the minute.

People who were afraid to lose their jobs if they reported through work channels would call Erik and tell him what they saw. They wanted another person to believe them and share their excitement and terror. Forest rangers, police, and others in positions to be called out to deal with the unexplained would call Erik and beg him not to use their name nor to publicize it. Some sightings would be so numerous, frequent, or brazen in an area that rangers would beg him to come and verify it.

People had personal reasons to want Erik to verify or follow up their sightings. If a "real expert in the field or authentic Bigfoot Hunter" came and agreed with them, it comforted them that they were not nuts. They might even have enough backup that not only were they not alone but they could now share the experienced with others and maybe even be acknowledged as a hero.

Around 1987, there was a UFO conference in Phoenix, Arizona. We stopped by to say hello to Jim Moseley who was way west of his usual haunt, Key West, Florida. We visited some attendee/friends in attendance.

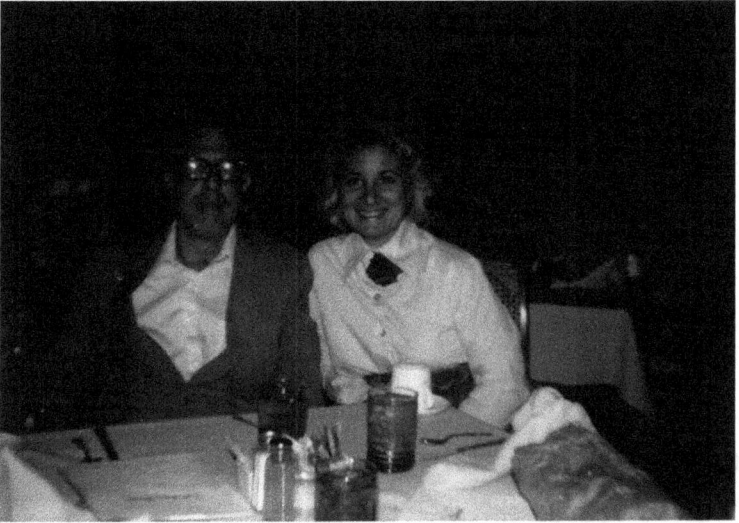

The Late Great Jim Moseley with Molly

We were on the way to investigate a cluster of Bigfoot sightings. We'd heard from some individuals and then from a ranger who was severely stressed describing what he had seen. He was desperate and felt the safety of one family with children was on the line. He said they were endangered and he did not know what he could do. Obviously, he felt he couldn't deal alone with what he was up against and urged Erik to come and see it. The family lived near the edge of the wilderness and they'd seen tracks and thought they'd seen a Bigfoot at least once. They called and reported it to the rangers. More tracks appeared over several days. The ranger kept checking the tracks but didn't know what to do. He told Erik that he'd be fired and disbelieved if he said he saw a Bigfoot but that he had to do something for that frightened family. He sounded stressed himself. We rarely went on bigfoot trips over a certain distance because of costs.

No one ever offers money. If you remember Erik's website, he had at the top something like "You don't do this for money."

Erik demurred going to investigate immediately because it was hundreds of miles to the next state and we did not have extra money at the time. The ranger was insistent and said he at least wanted an official Bigfoot hunter to back up what he'd seen. He didn't know how to get the Bigfoot to stop coming around the family's home. Erik thought of this family with little kids and decided to go. He said he didn't know what we could do if we ran into Bigfoot either. We packed the 1978 T-bird and drove off to Arizona. We stopped at Phoenix to visit Jim Moseley and others at the UFO convention then went on. Erik introduced me as "Miss Bigfoot Bait" to some new acquaintances.

Erik told Jim about the reports coming out of the ranger station. Many believe Bigfoot's related to UFO's somehow, so Erik told what we'd heard to Jim. Jim followed up later in "Saucer Smear" reporting to those investigators what we'd found. We drove about 80 miles north/northwest of Phoenix, if my directional memory is correct. We entered beautiful mountainous terrain. We passed where the ranger said activity was reported and passed the family's home. We went several miles more. Bigfoots could walk over terrain where the road was more circuitous. After a few more miles of fire road, we were passing a group of new pickup trucks being driven along the dirt road for off-road testing. When they found an area they could ride around in the dirt, they pulled off and we passed them. I saw some of them staring, certain we were nuts to be driving an old car so far into wilderness, prior to cell phones. Erik asked a lot of his vehicles in his searches. When Erik died, he had an SUV, well used. But, in 1987 We had the old Thunderbird. We drove until the fire road ended and then drove up a dry gravel creek bed as far as we could without getting the car stuck. This would have been a snow creek in winter or spring. A flash flood would've left us and the car in a hurt. Erik just hoped we'd get in and out of the forest and back to the car before it rained.

We opened the trunk, loaded up, tossing extra weight and equipment back into the open trunk. I'll always regret leaving the plaster. I did not believe in Bigfoot, even though I'd seen tracks before and understand you at least make a track cast as documentation if you find tracks. We were burdened by carrying all our camping equipment. I had my camera. Erik put the whistle around my neck later, after we were overwhelmed with the situational evidence. He told me to blow the whistle if we got separated and to take pictures with another camera he gave me and throw it down where I whistled.

I'm so sorry I don't have a track cast from that trip. We measured tracks, numbered them, noted directions, noted poop, (Erik pulled piles apart and recorded what diet appeared to be). I had planned to use my camera to take the pictures of wildflowers. I had humored Erik as he piled equipment into the car for a Bigfoot Expedition, a fanciful waste of time. Now, I'll never camp alone in a strange wood again in my life.

The view down, from the top of the mountain where we were, looked steep and far down. Erik said we'd slide down. We hadn't packed rappelling equipment. I was on a 3- or 4-day weekend and due back at school to teach after the weekend. We slid down on our backsides, descending at least 1,000 feet into a valley floor with tree covering. We picked ourselves up. I looked up at the way we'd come and said, "Boy, that's going to be some climb back up!"

Erik said "We're hiking out. I can't climb that or I'll have a heart attack." We started walking after Erik checked his map and compass and made some notes. After about 10-15 minutes we came to a pile of scat. Shortly thereafter we saw the first of many tracks. We didn't have plaster, so we measured it, measured the stride and counted the steps. I had Erik jump around and try to make as deep an impression. He obliged. He couldn't.

I just kept referring to the "unusual erosion patterns." The alternative, to voice what it looked like, knowing we were in totally unfamiliar territory miles away from any human company, would've voiced the unthinkable and acknowledged we were at the mercy of some large numerous unknown beings and possible predators (bear or Bigfoot). I didn't want to risk a psychotic breakdown.

The steps on one long trail we followed led up to a huge fallen tree, about 4 feet in diameter. One print of a left foot was in front of it. The other print, of the right foot, was on the other side of the huge fallen log. Yes, it looked as though something very Big had stepped over effortlessly continuing with the right foot track on the other side.

Twelve more foot prints led up to the opening through rock into a beautiful green, lush valley. The opening was a few feet wide, like a pass. A lot of tracks went into it.

The forest we'd come through had been abnormally silent and still. No small life forms moved in it. No squirrels, no birds, nothing small and edible was seen or heard. We were the smallest, it appeared.

I saw the numerous and varied foot size tracks, all large, going into that valley and thought "Wow!!! If I were a Bigfoot I'd want to live in there!"

Erik was all excited and said "Let's go!" and started in.

I said "Where?" and started in the opposite direction, Fast.

Erik pointed, In there!"

"No Way!" I took off in the opposite direction – that I hoped was OUT. I knew I had a long way to go. Erik tried to convince me to go through the pass. He Said I couldn't find my way alone. I said I'd follow the creek out and he could catch up, but that I didn't have the time. I had to be back teaching in a few days and it'd take time to get back.

I took off. Nothing was going to get me to voluntarily go through that opening. On the way, I'd smelled a stench more than once. When I looked at one spot of plants after Erik told me it was skunk cabbage I blinked because looking at the patch of green it looked like brown fur right behind it and between two plants. I slowly walked the three yards to it – not daring to look up from the patch about a yard up from the ground. I was staring almost nose to fur/hair/brown as I came up. I couldn't look up to the eyes. I did not want to look into eyes. If I looked into the eyes it would be able to look into my eyes and it might be moved to attack in some way. I looked up to the bottom of wide head and couldn't go farther. The fur melted backward until it was gone and the odor had moved. There was a patch of light between the plants now. I could look beyond a few feet. I was no longer about 4" from some being's belly. The maltese dog has hair instead of fur. I've petted and seen them. I am looking at Tinker asleep right now. This skin covering was hairlike not fur, not thick and rough like the collie. After that, Erik gave me a whistle to wear around my neck and his camera, not mine. He said take some pictures next time and throw the camera down. I was to blow the whistle where I tossed the camera down. That totally changed my attitude toward Erik. I never counted on him again. I was on my own. I moved out later and I did not accept his proposal of marriage.

Erik had discussed an article in a gossip newspaper telling about an Indian woman who'd allegedly been kidnapped by Bigfoot and eventually escaped. I now began limping to appear visibly deformed as well as runty-short. I would only appeal to a desperate Bigfoot pedophile. Erik walked quickly in front of me 20 to 30 feet with his back turned. I asked him to slow down but he wouldn't.

We saw some trees bent to form a little round hollow. Erik showed difference between this tree shaping and how bears bend and break young trees. As we were walking out, without entering the green passage, we saw more tracks. Erik said they were "old." Only back home did he say they were fresher, but he "didn't want to scare (me)." I was miserable on that trip. The fun of camping, photographing wildflowers, was eclipsed by terror. The route we took was dictated by my seeing so many footprints and having NO DESIRE to face huge hairy beings in their habitat. We turned north and away from the footprints. We were watched or monitored (followed) until we were past their watering hole, which had tons of tracks in a path. The night we camped out we had not reached the watering hole yet. Erik made a big fire, sat up awake, and kept yelling and jumping around. It occurs to me writing this, years later, that maybe he wasn't saying "come and take the woman in the tent" to Bigfoot. Maybe he was just doing all that because it is taught in Scouting and outdoor classes as techniques to scare or keep away wild animals. Twice I came out of the tent to tell him to stop and come to sleep. He sent me back and said "get back inside the tent."

The route to the water, I'd guess from the tracks, went around the south end, up, over the peak, and down slightly to this beautiful, pristine mountain pool about 20 to 30 feet across. We were sweaty messes by the time we got there, drank and washed. I told Erik we were polluting their drinking water. That was why there were so many footprints. He figured if he got them mad they'd show.

Our route took us to a very vertical canyon side, about 1/3 down the west face, the path getting narrower and narrower until we were clinging to the cliff face inching north on a 6" ledge. A goat couldn't have done it without body width pushing it off and falling waaay down to the bottom of the crevice, or narrow canyon. I was fighting gravity as I moved and I had no handhold and started tipping backwards twice. Erik's huge hand slammed me into the cliff. He did this while clinging to the rock himself. If I'd fallen, no one would've believed he didn't kill me and leave me in the wilderness.

We hiked out north – when we started getting to normal wilderness off the cliff, we were really relieved. This was late in the second day. After some miles we came to a site we recognized from one Bigfoot report. One road crew had been assigned to go "deep inland" from the highway. There was some small hut as I recall, where the men had spent a night. That night, they had been terrified by several Bigfoot throwing rocks at the hut roof and yelling around them. They fled in the morning and said they'd never go back to finish the project. I think a bridge had washed out or needed repair. It's hard to remember. But what the report had said was the edge of the wilderness" we laughed at. To us, it was a sign of human activity and we were at the edge of civilization.

When we got to the highway, we walked a ways to a beer bar, the first place we found. That beer was delicious. We were heroes or a novelty to the patrons. Erik persuaded one fellow to drive us back to our car – for a $20 bill. The man couldn't believe how far back he had to drive. He kept turning around and looking at me for confirmation each time Erik said "No, not here. Further." When we finally got to the car, he said if he'd known how far it was he wouldn't have brought us.

Erik said after that trip that he'd never do it again without a team of pack mules or horses and more people. I pointed out that horses couldn't come in around the cliff that we climbed along.

This would become the trip that Erik said the rest of his life was "the worst Bigfoot trip of my life." This was the first extended Bigfoot campout I'd been on. It would be a few days in the wilderness. I brought my camera because I was known to take good photographs of wild flowers, which I'd give as gifts to friends. That "wear the whistle" routine pretty much ended any long-term feelings of commitment I might have had toward Beckjord. After that, knowing I was being watched, I limped like crazy, struggling at the same time to keep up while Erik kept walking out in front of me so I was a target. I figured if I limped no healthy Bigfoot in his right mind would want me. This was shortly after the article in the National Enquirer had come out with a headline kind of like "Indian woman kidnapped by Bigfoot." That trip was hell and I never went on another overnight Bigfoot hunt with Beckjord.

Chapter Fifteen
Unknown Doesn't Mean Paranormal; Another Bigfoot Sighting; Balls of Lightening; Ogopogo.

Erik has swung toward the answer to Bigfoot as some paranormal phenomena. Listen to some analogies: I remember once when I was home alone in Malibu. A huge long snake came out of the side of the basement where I stored my clothes and where I went to get dressed. No one would anticipate that. No one ever saw that snake except for me. I grabbed a bathing suit off the clothes line and did not go near the snake. I called the fire department after animal control told me to call them. Animal control did not want to come. They said the fire department was closer. The fire department argued that it wasn't their job. I went back and forth on the telephone. Finally, when the snake was lying on the warm cement apron with it's head in the grass somewhere and its tail still through the basement door the fire department agreed to come after I'd told them how wide the cement apron was. Of course, minutes before the fire department came the snake seemed to sense their presence coming and hightailed it into the tall grass. I never saw the snake again. The fire department thought I was nuts. I still wonder if they all thought I made it up.

Just because something is infrequently viewed doesn't make it paranormal any more than a rare comet is paranormal. A friend, Stan, used to say the dryer "ate (his) socks." His wife, Doreen, thought it was a figure of speech and kept bawling him out every time a sock was missing from the wash. Several years after Stan died, the dryer quit. Doreen called the repairman. When the dryer was opened up, the repairman laughed and called Doreen. The dryer had at least nine socks, none matching, that had somehow been sucked out of the drum vortex and into the casing hinterlands. Doreen felt terrible because she doubted Stan and could not share the find with him. The socks were never paranormal.

The first time I saw Bigfoot was Fish Camp. The second time, I still denied it to myself until my nose was about 4 inches from Bigfoot's belly. The third time, I was on my honeymoon with Art. We were gassing up somewhere on the edge of civilization in British Columbia. I was trained to always scan the mountains, in case I'd see a bigfoot and know where to look, make note of the time of year, day, and note the sighting. The trees near the top of the mountain were pines, from the shape of the one on the left. Suddenly a tall wide dark two footed creature hurried from the bigger tree to another one on the right. Maybe by guesswork it may have been visible for fifty feet on the open snow, outlined in the open. I looked around. Everyone was going about their business. Art had his head and eyes downward, focused on the gas nozzle. I always felt that when life has special moments, we are sometimes given special signs or occurrences to add to our joy. We call them Blessings. I reveled in my blessing. If it were nowadays, I'd shout "Quick, Look!" and maybe several of us would have seen it and it would have lent credence to the sighting and existence of Bigfoot. Groups of Indians have testified that they saw Bigfoot, but their statements are discounted or interpreted as the results of smoking hallucinogens, even when the witnesses say they were going about their daily business. It is possible, if one believes the Bible, to consider that the demons who were spoken of as coming down to be "with the daughters of men" wanted to reprise that role post-flood. They couldn't become human again because of God's edict. They may cohabitate with some higher apes, as the blood and four different encounter hair samples might suggest. Those are physical evidence. In genetic genealogy the spit cells are accepted as physical evidence and used to categorize people's ethnicity. Surely if spit DNA counts, the physical hairs Erik turned in along with the blood count as actual physical evidence.

If demons inhabit some Bigfoot bodies, then it may explain the fact that more than once people have said Bigfoot hid when they were thinking of shooting him. Some speak of Bigfoot speaking in their heads. The morning of the second day, after that night in the woods, a Bigfoot sat in the bushes I wanted to use for a toilet. I knew he was there. I walked around, giving the bushes a wide berth and wondering if I could get back to camp fast enough if he came out. I went in some rocks that looked like they were far enough from the river, but I couldn't get much higher, the canyon was steep. The Bigfoot sounded mad and asked why I "didn't go in the bushes."

I said "Because you are there." It spoke in my head. I got the feeling that it was nonplussed by my answer. It did not think people could know where it was. Speaking in my head was like it communicated thoughts without having to know a language. It spoke English, my language. I got mad and told him if he wanted me to go in the bushes, he shouldn't have been there.

Other Anomalies

Balls of light.

A friend was flying once, in a passenger seat by the wing. She looked out and saw lightening hit the end of the wing. The lightening rolled into a ball and kept rolling toward her. She had been warned in the past to make sure she was touching no part of the plane's fuselage if she ever saw "ball lightening" but to keep her hands on her seat and be only touching that. The lightening vanished just before it hit the hull. Many pilots are familiar with it. Don't touch the fuselage. She hugged her cushion.

Ogopogo

At Lake Okanagan, in eastern British Columbia, the Indians have had a legend for generations that a large lake monster dwells in the lake. The lake is about 30-35 miles long. Locals insist that in rainy season it's 100 miles long with numerous side tributaries. This would potentially give a wide ranging area to a water dweller. One time, Erik got an excited telephone call and subsequent mailed photographs from a man who insisted he'd seen something large in the lake. Erik showed me the photos and asked my opinion. He said he couldn't make out enough to have a conclusive opinion of whatever the photo showed. It was something dark, black shadow, rising out of the water. I couldn't tell if it was a tree stump, upended boat, or rock. We couldn't make out what it was.

M'kole M'Bembe at Lake

I remember one researcher in contact with Erik who said they saw something big and scary at an African lake. They couldn't get the natives to hang around. The researcher was in danger of being left in the jungle alone, so he came out with the natives.

Chapter Sixteen
UFO Happenings
UFO Abductee Implant

Erik was the photographer for the filmed removal of an alleged implant/foreign object less than one inch in size, fairly flat, rather v shaped, similar shape to shark's tooth. The object was said to be put there by the aliens who abducted the person. Erik paid out of his own pocket for the best quality film. Erik ran two cameras, to cover all camera angles during the operation. Erik showed the good quality film to the surgeon for whom he had made the film. Erik reported angrily that the man grabbed the good film and destroyed it. This left only the cheaper film. Erik swung and hit the man in the jaw. Erik had professional standards and would do his best, no matter what the outcome. Maybe the man thought Erik was going to steal his thunder or release it on his own.

Erik and Jim Moseley

Over twenty years ago, Erik and Jim used to talk regularly on the phone. Jim's main interest since the 1950s was UFO's. His newsletter "Saucer Smear" was the longest running UFO related publication. Erik came up with the name for the newsletter. Erik said it was mostly gossip about people in the UFO field. When Jim was trying on various titles, Erik suggested Saucer Smear. Maybe it was in the 1960's per Erik. Erik said he pointed out to Jim that it was mainly about UFO field gossip so "Saucer Smear" would be apropos. Jim liked it.

Years later, Erik was trying to raise money for another Loch Ness expedition. He got the idea of hitting up Jim for payment for use of the title "Saucer Smear." Jim was understandably really mad. He called Erik an extortionist or something similar and a few other terms. Erik was capable of real obstinacy if he thought it might advantage him or his arguments. He ran a friendship into the ground. Too bad, because Jim lived remarkably like Erik. Jim hunted down artifacts, especially in Peru, like Indiana Jones (only way before the movie). Then, Jim managed a small apartment building he owned, lived in Key West because he liked it, wouldn't move or marry Anna, his long-time female companion, and pursued UFOs as an avocation. Jim also had antiquities from Peru and other parts of South America. He sold them as he needed for money.

Erik had a five-shelf bookcase of VHS videos. Most appeared to be UFO, with Bigfoot, Nessie, and Crop Circles thrown in. There were other videos scattered around, but you have to see that Erik and Jim together were better for the UFO field. When Erik shared the videos, Jim could go investigate them. Many people sent Erik tapes of things they'd filmed, anomalies, TV shows from the USA or UK or Japan. Good wishes and notes were written on the covers of some. In Erik's files were neatly alphabetized files of reports, some with photos. But Erik did not usually investigate UFOs. He quit sending things to Jim. Jim had always been the pipeline of information in the UFO field.

People around the world sent Erik videos and stories of UFO sightings. Some of the NASA (National Aeronautics and Space Administration) tapes show balls of energy shooting toward the earth or even away from it. It reminds me of the scripture in Job where angels are mentioned as going to and from the earth. Most people recognize angels as a form of energy, spirit but not matter unless they choose to appear. The NASA tape with the balls of light ascending and descending to earth reminded me of that scripture. The tape recording was from a satellite or the space station. I can't remember.

Walter Blaney, a magician known as "Zaney Blaney," once was driving around his home state of Texas or somewhere nearby through desolate land. He and his daughters and wife all saw a UFO, something in the air that shown super bright lights on their car. Whatever it was, military or not, Walter felt he'd seen a UFO.

In the early days of space exploration, NASA called Walter in to see if he somehow knew a secret way to defy gravity. Walter levitated a woman onstage.

You laugh. Remember that Erik was seriously looking for mermaids. And National Geographic still sent out another explorer to seek mermaids after Erik.

UFO Reports

(Erik): I began getting stories of UFOs looking like footballs cruising over Bellingham Bay. But, personally, I did not see any.

Either this was a response to Erik's Crop Circle Welcome in the UK or another place. I can't remember.

Ilkley Moor

One photo of an alleged alien is the Ilkley Moor photo. Erik went to the UK a number of times. He made friends with locals and hired them to help out in the field. Erik tramped and boated around Loch Ness a number of times. When not in Scotland, Erik was in the south of England studying crop circles or anomalous occurrences like Ilkey Moor. Someone sent Erik a copy of a photograph they'd taken on Ilkey Moor. It was supposed to be a photograph of a strange form of life. It is bipedal, short, and supposedly the left arm is longer than the right. Erik makes much of the fact that the left hand is unusually long and not the same length as the right. I have read pages of analysis of this photograph and how it is an alien, must be an alien, and the glow of tubes is clearly visible on its chest. Remember that when we enlarge photographs there is space between the colored dots of the film. It can make the pattern confusing or introduce "noise" into the main subject matter of the photograph. Step back a bit or shrink this photo and you have what might be the outline at a distance of a small girl carrying a basket in her left hand. A bush is behind part of her head in the photograph. Small white flecks are evenly spaced down her chest, like buttons catching the sunlight and reflecting the light. It is hard to discern the truth when one gets too eager to find something exciting.

119

M. A. Squire, PhD

Erik's weakness was blowing up photos and getting them so enlarged that you couldn't see the overall shape and call it from your clear view, no matter how small it appears in the photo. The following is, to my knowledge, from Erik's stash sent to him to evaluate, from the internet.

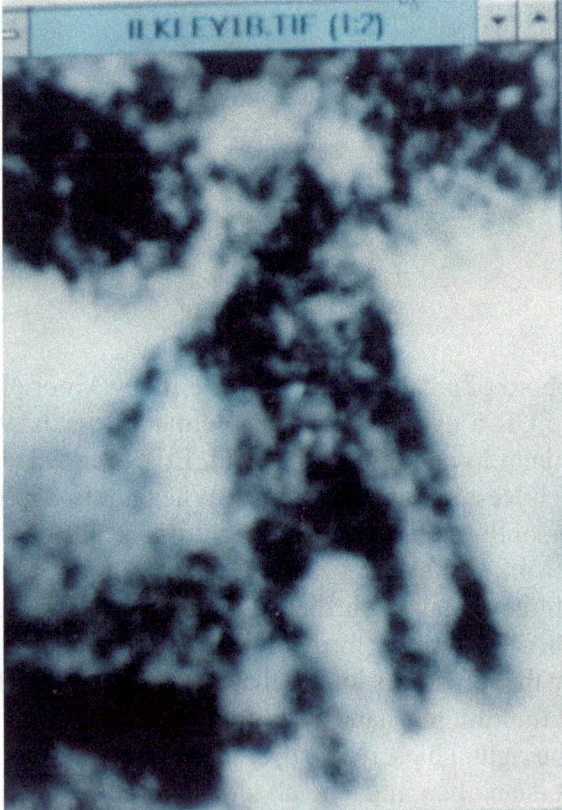

The Ilkley Moor photo

Chapter Seventeen
Crop Circles; Loch Ness

Crop Circles are associated with UFOs for those who believe beings in UFOs make the patterns in the growing crop to communicate with humans. Shapes and geometric designs that are sizes covering acres of growing grain appeared in the United States and the United Kingdom. In Saucer Smear, Jim Moseley did not appear to follow up on reports of crop circles although he reported the sightings. Jim did not investigate. Erik went to the UK for crop circle investigations. Once, Erik had a team in the field, with a farmer's consent, to create an outgoing message of friendship. They made a picture. I think I remember it was a "happy face." When a message was found in a crop about two days later, not in the same place but nearby, Erik interpreted it as friendly and a direct answer to the outgoing message.

Erik photographed crop circles, went up in a plane or helicopter to view some, discussed them in the local pubs, discussed them with people who took it seriously as strange phenomena, and generally gave his interpretations of what he thought the symbols might mean. As with Bigfoot and the Patterson Film, Erik went with a team to see if they could make crop circles and designs like those claimed to be from extraterrestrials, to see how likely such things were to be from unhuman beings.

Hanging out in the pub in the evenings was fun, too.

Workers came out to help Erik. He was good-natured
and could always poke fun at himself.

Loch Ness

When Erik wasn't exploring Loch Ness himself, he was in touch with other researchers trying to find or disprove the existence of Nessie, the Loch Ness Monster. The first photo of what was said to be the Loch Ness Monster was taken by a physician in the 1930's. Other photos have tried to prove or disprove the existence. There used to be a friendly seal that visited a local town on the Loch. Some years ago, some idiot killed it. We suspected it was someone who did not want it mistaken for the monster, if there was one. In the past, Nessie was sought by one researcher who coordinated a team of at least 20 boats to sweep the Loch systematically, in a line. Supposedly, if they started at one end and swept through to the other, they would come across Nessie. There were spaces between the boats. The lead researcher used a sonar sweep to read anything moving in the water. The waters of Loch Ness are cloudy and hard to see in. Divers don't like to go into the waters. While the boats were sweeping the Loch, something going very fast shot under the research boat at a depth of about 600 feet. Erik was on the telephone with the lead researcher. They were both excited. The lead researcher decided not to mention the anomaly to the press, because he did not know what it could be. He said it was way too deep to be the seal. Erik went a few years later and set up a camera to film in the direction of the speeding anomaly. He set the cameras to work automatically from a high shoreline area. This gave him plenty of time to go visiting and pubbing before he'd head back to change out the film and play the recent roll to see if he got something. He Did Get Something. There is something swimming in the water making a "V" wake. It is not a boat wake. Erik enlarged the picture. It seems to show a face. Whether it was a seal or not or showed a long body due to the wake length, as Erik claimed, is arguable. This is probably one reason some person around there shot the seal sometime after that.

I remember seeing an article years ago in Life Magazine. It discussed Loch Ness and showed an underwater photograph of a diamond shaped fin brushing past a diver. It seemed to have a big body attached to it. The picture was matched to a picture of a dinosaur called a plesiosaur. They fit.

Erik knew divers who refused to ever get back into the water. They were very shaken. They said they felt a big body brush by them. Accounts from around 600 A.D. tell of a man being rescued from the mouth of the monster by the interference of St. Columbo.

Erik made numerous trips to Loch Ness. I was there with Art. We were driving out of the Loch Ness area, heading south, going up the road up the hill out of the area. I turned around, with the video recorder on the back seat of the car, and I looked in a small area nearby where Erik had said sightings occurred. I saw a small black island rise, rounded. I debated getting the recorder but felt that if I did I would lose sight of the phenomena. I kept watching. Art was in no place to pull over and look. I reported to him. As he drove, I watched the island slowly go under the surface when we hit the top of the grade. Scientists have suggested that there is nothing in the water. They suggest that any anomaly is a rotten log rising with gas. This was not log shaped. If it rose with gas it must have discharged the gas and went down again.

Drumnadroicht is a small town at Loch Ness. It is Erik's favorite for setting up camp. He used to camp in a "caravan" or small "trailer" to Americans. Erik's last trip produced a video of something long and tubular swimming in the loch. The photos, film, all video was sent to the China Flats Cryptozoological Repository for categorizing and making available to researchers around the world.

Erik's report, with optical physicist Bruce Maccabbee, on Loch Ness:

Unusual Photographs From Loch Ness
J. E. Beckjord and Bruce S. Maccabee, Ph.D.

Introduction

A Team from the National Cryptozoological Society (NCS) of the U.S.A. conducted a seven day photographic surveillance expedition at Loch Ness, Scotland, between July 29-Aug. 4th, 1987. The expedition was headquartered at the Achnahannet caravan site, two miles toward Fort Augustus from Urquhart Bay, and just across from Inverfarigaig. The primary purpose was to take 16mm film footage of boats to verify the scale relationships of a film taken by the NCS from the same location in 1983. The secondary goal was to obtain additional film or still shots of the unusual object that was recorded in 1983. And the third goal was a study of the 1981 Jennifer Bruce photograph site so as to determine how close the object in her photo was to the shore and the actual size of the mooring buoys in her photo. In all three areas, the expedition produced interesting results.

A Low-Budget Expedition

Since the expedition was on a tight budgetd it consisted of only two persons – J.E. Beckjord and Mr. Alex Crosbie of Edinburgh.

Mr. Crosbie proved to be a valuable asset to the expedition. The fieldwork consisted of visual surveillance using binoculars of 10 x and 50 x, a mirror-relex telescope of 1000 mm., and a night-vision device, made by Litton Industries, model M841. Photographic equipment included a Bolex Rex IV 16 mm camera, with 400 mm lens, a Beaulieu super 8 mm camera, a Eumig underwater super 8 mm camera, a Polaroid 190 folding camera, two 35 mm SLR cameras with one 270 mm telephoto lens, and Mr. Crosbie's 110 pocket camera.

Using the Bolex,, the first day, July 29, was spent filming various boats in the loch from the same spot that the 1983 film had been taken. The same site, camera and lens were used. The weather conditions were identical, and the Loch was mirror calm. The time was the same (8 a.m.). Following this work, Beckjord left for Inverness to get a hire-car, while Crosbie maintained watch, with a 35 mm camera, pre-set, ,at his side. Upon the return of Beckjord, later that evening, Crosbie informed him that he had taken several shots of a disturbance in the water near several passing boats, which later proved to be the 40 foot motor sailer Emenoyi, and the 37 foot rental cruiser Silver Spirit I. In the following days the weather proved to be spotty and difficult for surveillance, so the team used the time to process the film and to search for the crews of the two boats. In addition, other researchers such as Richard Raynor, who had filmed an object in the loch in 1967, were interviewed. On July 31, the photos were developed at the Boots chemist's shop in Inverness. On August 1, buoy measurements were made with the help of Mr. Gorden Menzies, owner of the Temple Pier Marina. On August 3, the framing of the Bruce photo was established. On August 4th, merganser ducks were studied in the River Ness and on August 5th, the expedition returned to Edinburgh and then to London. After five days there (in London) a flight was taken back to the U.S.

Results

One hundred feet of 16 mm footage was obtained of cruisers and sailboats at the 1983 film site. Based on these, a size of ten feet for the object seems proper for the 1983 film. Mr. Crosbie obtaned seven 35 mm stills in color negative (400 asa) and four stills in 110 color negative of an object in the loch at a range of 1000 yards. The stills were taken over an estimated period of twenty minutes, with the 35 mm stills taken outdoors, and the 110 stills taken from inside the caravan, through a window. The time was 4:50 pm, with the sun behind Crosbie and to his right, and still relatively high in the sky, with no clouds in most shots and under flat conditions. Mr. Crosbie reported that at 4:50 pm, he had stood outside and noted a water disturbance leading to a possible collision with the first boat, the Emenoyi. He watched the object, which seemed to resemble a spike, creating a wakee which crossed in front of the boat, and then, using the pre-set camera, he took the first three photos, no. 9, 10, and 11. These show the object making a left turn, going away from the bboat. Photo no. 9 shows the wake widening out during the turn, photo no. 10 shows a gradual lengthening of the wake into a narrow wake, and photo no. 11 shows a resumption of straight line travel, still to dthe left, creating a narrow wake. Mr. Crosbie had used 20 power binoculars, so there is littlek reason to doubt he saw a spike (average binoculars are a mere 7X). The Emenoyi then left the area and the water calmed back down to mirror flatness. After perhaps ten minutes more, Crosbie again noted the object n the water, this time moving toward Fort Augustus, to the right, and with no bots close to it. He then took shots no. 12 and 13. In these two photos, the body of the object appears to be at the surface. A few minutes later, Mr. Crosbie noted that the cruiser Silver Spirit I was approaching, and he photographed the long object doing evasive action to avoid this boat, in photos no. 14 and 15. Once the cruiser had passed, Mr. Crosbie went inside the caravan, and through a window, took four photos. These photos are less clear than the 35 mm photos that he took from outside the caravan, and are not shown here. These photos were nos. 20, 21, 22, and 23. The first three (20-22) show boats on the loch in the general direction of Dores and Inverness, and the last photo, no. 23, shows the loch area just to the right of Achnahannet, with Inverfarigaig visible. In this photograph, there may appear the long moving object that was recorded in the 35 mm photos, but this is very much open to interpretation, due to the lack of fine definition inherent in 110 cameras. This photo does show the next logical areaa beyond the area of photos 12, 13, 14, and 15, toward Fort Augustus, where the object might have gone through. Over all, the duration of the photography did not exceed 20 minutes according to Mr. Crosbie.

Crosbie also reported that he is familiar with ducks, loons, mergansers and various water birds, for he had worked aroud the loch for many years as a laborer for the Inverness Public Works Department, and had spent much time outdoors. He feels that the spike he saw initially was not a loon nor any other waterbird.

Comments and Analysis by Bruce Maccabee, Ph.D.

Seven color photos with selected enlargements were sent to me between January 1988 and April 1988 by the C.M.P. After spending a considerable amount of time in analysis, I determined the following:

1.   The object in the photos shows an extra-ordinary object, something not expected to be found in lakes based on my experience as to what is normal for lake waters.

2.   The object was located in Loch Ness, some 1000 yards from the camera with the camera located 216 feet over the lake level.

3.   The object does not appear to be based on wind in various fauna indigenous to lakes in general. It is not a model nor a submarine.

4.   The photos show two different types of swimming behavior by the object.

5.   Photos 9, 10, & 121 show rapid movement of an object that seems submerged with a projection creating arrow wake. This object is heading left, and avoiding a boat.

6.   Photos 12, 13, 14, & 15 show more languid movement, with a generalized tubular shape of perhaps 48 feet, with a head at one end that seems roughly shield-shaped. The body is at the surface.

7.   In photos 12 and 132, this tubular object is moving to the right.

8.   In photos 14 and 15, the object turns, away from another boat, toward the bottom of the photo.

9. The object in photo 13 has a plume-like projection in front of it that may or may not be the same type of plume that can be seen in photo no. 15. This is conjectural.

10. The object has a flexible body that may have a variable thickness, with possibly a thicker area close to the head portion in some photos. This is open to interpretation.

11. The body may be yellow to yellow-brown.

12. Any details in the head area may be a fortuitous combination of color film grains, and are subject to individual interpretation.

Comments and Analysis by J. E. Beckjord

I generally agree with the statements by Dr. Maccabee, that the object is tubular, variable in diameter, above the surface in the last four photos, and below the surface in the first three. Mr. Crosbie reported that he had seen a spike creating the narrow wake just before he snapped the photos and this seems consistent with the first three photos. I agree that the object is extra-ordinary, and Charles Wyckoff has stated on the telephone that the object is indeed very extra-ordinary.[i]

I further agree that the object is not the kind of thing that is normally found in such lakes. No known fauna from lakes, nor common objects such as logs, algae mats, seaweed, models, submarines, etc., are responsible. I see the object as being reddish-brown to yellow, in different photos. As a personal interpretation, subject to differing opinions, I feel the plume in photo 13 is the same type as in photo no. 15. One might speculate that this could possibly be water vapor, or something similar to the spout of a whale. I agree with Maccabee that the object has a shield-shaped head and that the tubular body is at the surface and represents a body, not a water disturbance. Further in this report, there will be presented some comments and opinions by various zoologists who have viewed these photos, regarding what possible animals these photos may, or may not, show. In regard to Dr. Maccabee's statement concerning the details of the head area of the object, I feel that there is more detail to be found that may be significant, and that furthermore, the details of this head area tend to match in many respects in all seven photos. However, more research and enlargement is required to document such alleged details, and that is best presented in another paper at some future date. All of the statements above are my personal opinions and do not reflect the opinion of the journal.

The photos were enlarged by Beckjord at a lab in Santa Monica, and at the Producers Photo Lab in Hollywood, where the staff immediately noted the strange object in each shot. The results were shown in 4" x 6" form to the staff of the Los Angeles County Museum of Natural History and Harvey Fischer of the Los Angeles Zoo. Larger photos in 5" x 7" were shown to the associate curator of birds at the zoo, Mike Cunningham. All of the above have since been sent 5x7s and enlargements of the "head" area in photos no. 14 and 15. The reaction on the part of the LACMNH staff, Dr. John Heyning and Jeff Siegal (Marine Mammals, Fishes), was that the object was not a whale, porpoise, manatee, seal, otter, deer or dog. Siegal did suggest that back of a salmon, however, it should be noted that showing its back for over ten minutes and creating a long 48-foot trail or wake is very unsalmon-like in a 1000 deep foot lake. Salmon do display their backs when spawning in shallow streams where clearance is limited. Harvey Fischer, Herptology, states that the object "was not a snake." Mike Cunningham, Ornithology, noted that the wider object at the head of the object was reddish-brown, and was much thicker than the mast on the boat (2 inches), and that it had two large eyes. His conclusion was that the object definitely was not a loon, nor a cormorant, nor any other type of duck or waterbird. He cited the width (four to five times the mast), the large eyes, the color and the wake, plus lack of any bird body over such a long period. Mr. Jim Lecky and one other staff member of the National Marine Fisheries Service (USDofC) could not identify the object as anything known to them. Another zoologist, the head of the biology department at California State University at Los Angeles, David Soltz, Ph.D., has viewed the photo series in

February 1988, and says "The object is not a salmon, and I agree that salmon only show their backs mainly in shallow water when spawning. It also does not look like any fish that I know of, and the water pattern this object leaves is not typical of the kind that a fish would leave. I also do not feel that it is an otter, nor a seal nor a porpoise." Dr. Soltz also said that he would have no hesitation in verifying what he said should he be contacted. At the same institution, Dr. Carlos Robles stated that the object was not an invertebrate, which would eliminate squid, and he recommended that experts on hydro-dynamics be consulted in regard to the unusual wake pattern.

In photos 9, 10, & 11 there is a narrow wake which at first appears to widen out as a turn is made, but which becomes narrow again once the turn is finished. Ducks (except loons that are half-submerged), otters, dogs, deer, seals, and manatees all create a wide vee-wake when swimming. Periscopes, pipes, and semi-submerged loons can create narrow wakes, but in the case of loons, such a wake can end suddenly with submergence and diving ducks usually do not swim on the surface for long periods without diving for fish. Mergansers tend to dive continually and spend not more than several seconds on the surface.

Of special interest is the fact that in 1975, Carol Rines (Mrs. Robert Rines) of the Academy of Applied Sciences, took several still photographs from the Rines home (Tychat) located high over Urquhart Bay of two moving objects in the water that were moving parallel to each other. The photos, taken via a very powerful Questar Lens, show two narrow wakes, headed by what appears to be possibly a pair of projections or horns, one pair at the head of each wake.

Of further interest is that these new 8 photos were taken frm the very same spot as was the 1983 fillm. Mr. Crosbie is not a professional photographer, and he did not know until just an hour before leaving Edinburgh that he was to be part of the Expedition. Neither Beckjord nor Crosbie knew until one hour before arrival, that the Achahannet site would be their headquarters (HQ). Under these circumstances, it seems unlikely that Mr. Crosbie had any time to enlist confederates, even had he been inclined to do so.

Mr. Crosbie is 65 years old, and is an unsophisticated man.

Contact with the owners or renters of the two boats was made, and neither had seen any object while going by. Each stated that they had been in a rush, or had been looking at the hills around the loch and not at the water.

In regard to the Bruce photo, which shows a head and neck close to some buoys off Temple Pier, the buoys were determined to have been 24 inches in size, thus giving the object a height of from 5-6 feet and verifying Dr. Stors Olsen's judgment (Smithsonian, Curator of Birds) that the object in the photo was not any kind of bird, or waterbird. The framing of the photo would indicate that the object was quite close to the land by the Temple Pier lay-by where Ms. Bruce had been in 1981. The distance appears to have been some fifty feet from the shore. The Bruce photo had been taken with a 110 camera, and a similar camera was used to establish the framing. 35 mm and 110 photos were taken for comparison.

Future Plans

Computer enhancement does not seem called for in this case, only better and sharper enlargements in color. It is planned to compare these photos from 1987 with the 1983 Film, with the 1967 Raynor Film, the 1936 Irvine Film and other films as may be obtained. Additional optical and zoological experts will be contacted, as well as hydrologists who are expert on water movements. At the present time, the indications are that a new type of creature or object has been photographed that does not match any of the usual species of land or water animals that are indigenous to Loch Ness.

Another expedition is planned for 1988, involving Mr. Crosbie, to see if he can repeat his achievement. While it may not be possible to establish a new species of creature by photography alone, a series of matching and consistant images will encourage the search to go on. Of particular interest is that Operation Deepscan, a large organized sonar sweep of Loch Ness, produced one solid sonar reading in early October.. This reading was taken just one mile from the location of these new photographs.

J. E. Beckjord, MBA
18711 PCH, Malibu, CA 90265

Bruce Maccabee, PhD
10706 Meadowhill Rd.
Silver Spring, MD 20907

Urquhart Castle at Loch Ness centuries ago, from a woodcut, Dorothy Donofrio, artist.

Chapter Eighteen
Lake Okanagan

Lake Okanagan is east of Vancouver, in British Columbia, Canada. The lake is said to be 30-35 miles long. A local insists it is 100 miles long counting tributaries filling it with water. The local Indians say that Ogopogo lives in the lake and that some have seen it. The stylized statues and sculptures in parks and around town seem to indicate that Ogopogo is shaped like Nessie. Erik went to Lake Okanagan but saw nothing. Then, he received a photograph from someone swearing they had taken the picture at Lake Okanagan. They said it was a picture of something in the water. They claimed they thought it was Ogopogo. Erik asked me what it looked like to me. I said "a tree stump in water." He had to agree that he had tried hard to picture something alive, but it appeared to be a stump.

British Columbia Bigfoot

Art and I were getting gas at a gas station well out of Vancouver. We were near some very high, huge mountains that still had snow on them. It was the end of June, 1990. I was used to scanning the landscape to look for Bigfoot. I stood and scanned the mountains, in the trees, in the snow, near the top, while Art gassed the car. One big dark bipedal went quickly from one tree to the next. It crossed an expanse of snow. It was big because it was high up on the tree and I could see it from the gas station down in the valley. It was shaped like Bigfoot, not a big, four-footed moose or deer. That was the third time in my life I saw Bigfoot.

Mount Elvis

Erik is the only person I know who had a copy of a frame of the Patterson Film with NOT the Bigfoot circled but "faces" he saw in the background noise of the light and shadow in the photo. Toward the end, Erik lost the ability to write, his small cryptic jagged hand broke into a zigzag like an earthquake seismograph chart. So, he documented in the way he could. He photo'd any place he saw a face. Get this: a face can be two dots with a third one somewhere next to them, toward the center. See how easy it was for him to see faces? At the very end, Erik had lost the ability to write. He couldn't sign his normal signature. So, he relied on his old camera more. He took photos of a picture of a ship in his bedroom, hanging it at different angles and snapping photos. He claimed he could see faces at different angles.

It was a tragedy that a man who carefully filed and labelled everything lost his ability to write. How frustrating. He had me give him a spiral bound notebook so he could keep busy until the end. But, in the end Erik lost his ability to write. His pancreatic cancer somehow had destroyed his small motor control in his hands. He couldn't write. Six 5 drawer file cabinets (my notes say 6 but I remember it as 9) filled with labelled folders, all alphabetical. Notes to himself tacked up around his house as long as I knew him. Goals listed and stuck to the refrigerator. He was a great believer in visualization to achieve a goal. For 3 or 4 years he had a photo of a boat on his refrigerator until at last, he owned a sailboat.

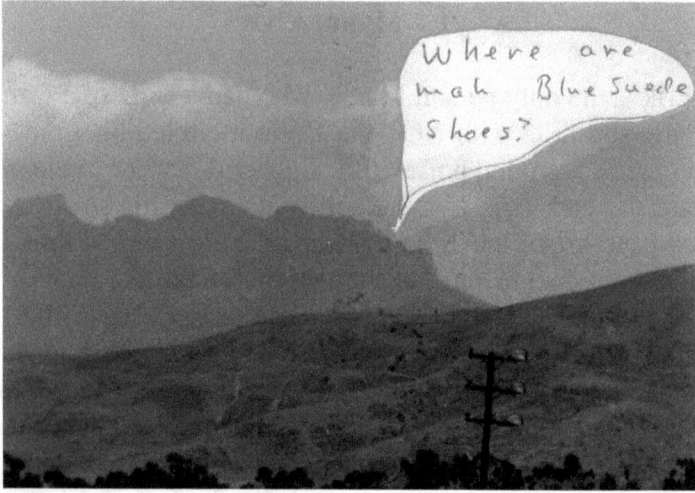

One of the many faces Erik saw in nature was "Mount Elvis" where Erik wrote the words "Where are mah Blue Suede shoes?" (A reference to a favorite early song of Elvis Presley.) He saw humor in many places.

La Fayette

Erik's last place to live, prior to the last days in a loving care hospice house, was in La Fayette, California. In the front yard was an oak tree with a plaque telling how many hundreds of years old the tree was and that it was the first one in the valley. The house was listed as one of 4 or 5 old adobes remaining in the whole valley. The living room had a big whitewashed rounded chimney in one corner. The house rambled under its tile roof, alone at the top of a hill. But the home was just down enough from the peak not to be visible from the main road running alongside the hill. On the street side stood the La Fayette Crosses, over 4,000 at last count, with names, one for each soldier who had died in the Iraq War.

When Erik first saw the house, it had been stripped of old fixtures while vacant, was loaded with cobwebs, grunge, dirt poured into the kitchen sink pipes, broken plumbing, and dead electrical circuits. He methodically repaired and cleaned out drains and pipes until the systems were functional.

Erik was an Eagle Scout with about 68 merit badges. I saw his sash years ago It must've burnt in the Malibu fire of 1993. The scouting background helped Erik repair, make-do, feel comfortable in the woods. The part of the scout law that says a scout is thrifty really sank in.

Laurie

Laurie Lawrence was Beckjord's last girlfriend, a stunning brunette who looked like Wonder Woman. She followed him up to the Bay Area (San Francisco and surrounds, East Bay, etc.). She was a lovely woman. She cooked a good Thanksgiving dinner. Laurie had a place with a small backyard in Richmond, the San Francisco Bay area, and continued her main income as a cold call vitamin salesperson. She was very good. The voice on the phone that sounds like it's a good-looking woman really was true in her case. Laurie was a doll, as sweet as she was pretty. She complained of pains in her legs and the doctor prescribed a medication. He neglected to tell her not to have alcohol with it. She sat in front of the television every work night with her glass of wine. After two days of not seeing her, around November 6, 2006, her neighbor called Erik to check on her. He found her dead in bed. She hadn't read the directions not to combine the medicine with alcohol. Erik rescued her birds and took care of them for about six months until he could find a fellow Mensan going to the Los Angeles area. He paid the Mensan friend to get the birds to me for my mom. He felt happier knowing Mom was caring for the last living link with Laurie. He rescued her birds, Cheep and Meep. He was anxious to tell Mom to push a button on a dangling musical attachment on the fancy cage. It played the melody "My Favorite Things" from the "Sound of Music." Erik was certain it would comfort the birds as Laurie used to play it for them.

Laurie had said she'd leave everything to Erik, because she didn't want to leave her father a "cent." She hadn't written the will or it was never found. Her insurance went to her father.

She had two parakeets, Laurie got leg pains, was taking a medicine for them, drank wine, and had a heart attack.

Erik's Museums

Erik had the Trancas Corners Museum, then a Marina Del Rey one after the Malibu Fire. When he moved north, he opened a San Francisco Museum. The following photograph shows one boy in the crowd who came to the big opening of the UFO-Bigfoot Museum in San Francisco. Notice some of the track casts. Some had been lost in the Malibu Fire.

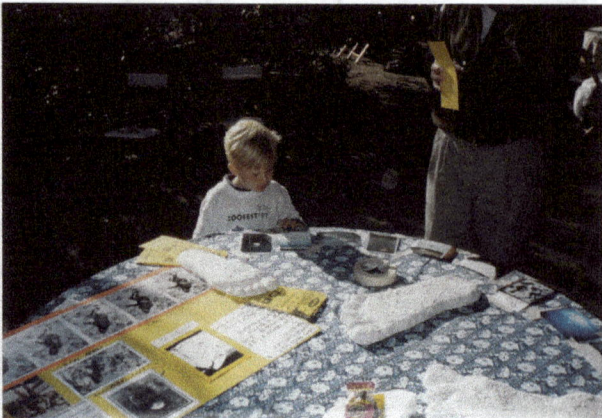

Ghost Busting

Erik and I were advertised as ghost busters. If you had a problem you thought might be paranormal, you could call and tell us about it. If we thought it sounded interesting, we'd solve your problem. One call came in from a resident of a dorm at the University of Southern California. I saved the letter of thanks after we were done. All we asked was that a letter of thanks be written to us on the USC stationery. We got a call about a haunted basement. The managers had taken to locking the room and wouldn't let anyone into it. Two or three young female students had taken to hanging out in the room on Saturday nights when they were dateless. They would shut off the lights. We showed up to solve the issue of the cold and the ghost that showed up. They had unwittingly been practicing sensory deprivation. It helped them feel disoriented. We arrived with thermometers, cameras, breeze measuring apparatus, and more equipment that apparently impressed the heck out of some students with no dates that evening. Erik and I set everything up. We recorded every 15 minutes. We noted where the draft came from. We told the young impressionable observers where to sit and stay out of the way. We turned out the lights and heard their gasps. There was a glow coming from one part of the large room. I started tiptoeing toward it in the dark. Imagine a closet with no windows. It was a dark basement. I felt and heard the quiet shuffle behind me. No one wanted to sit alone where we had put them. They wanted to be behind me. It was flattering to think they thought of me as a capable human shield, but I knew better. I approached the glow. The quiet shuffle behind me stopped a distance away. I touched the glow. Then I had the lights turned on. The ceiling was patched with enamel glossy white paint. The rest of the ceiling was non-glossy. The glow was from the light under one of the doors which just bounced enough to light up the patch on the ceiling. The written report went out and we received our thank-you letter.

Another time we were called as ghost busters was by a radio show. Erik was the believer, impressionable, not discarding any theory. I was the cut and dried hardcore "show me" buster. The radio show host wanted us back and said we were great and played against each other. Callers would call in with their issues and we'd suggest things or tell what it sounded like over the telephone. We could not afford to scamper off to everyone who decided they needed a ghost buster.

Roswell, New Mexico

Erik went out to Area 51. He used binoculars and tried to see what he could. He concluded on his last trip out that they had moved the actual area of operations and were maintaining just enough activity to sidetrack observers.

Washington on Mars

Erik made the famous discovery that when Mars was viewed through a telescope it appeared to have George Washington's face on it. Many of us remember this all over the news. It was touted as potential evidence of a past civilization on Mars. It was the result of shadows of some canyons on the surface of the planet. The photos are used today in science exhibits to capture the imagination and for entertainment.

Later

The La Fayette house was a typical find of Erik's. People would wonder how he "lucked out" and found homes they wanted to live in. Most people don't look with vision. They only see what's in front of them. They can't picture the "what if" and they don't have the skills and competencies to fix things. It used to be said that Italians enjoy working with their hands. I find that competent people usually master more than one skill. When they are older, they have flexed in life enough to fit into various fields and to address whatever they came across. Erik was the end result of Eagle Scout Doing and higher intelligence combined with a love of hands-on and a willingness to do whatever it took to accomplish a goal. Nowadays, it is harder to find people willing to get their hands "dirty." Even the expression shows contempt for manual labor. Erik, Art and I always admired competence.

Ineffectualness is not sexy. Skill is sexy. Hands-on is sexier than an all-day desk job. Thus, my nephew and niece Robert and Rebecca Crouch are a sexy couple. They drive truck as a team. This is hands-on tons of steel. The ultimate measure of success is that they deliver goods safely. But they have shown me horrible videos that show how an instant's gust of wind can flip an empty semi-truck.

Today's young people are trying to measure each other's competency in introductions that always include "I'm working on a game…" or some variant of that. This is what passes for being under the car hood "tinkering" like you knew what you were doing, in the 1950's.

The last home Erik was in, on top of a hill, hidden from view by greenery, was similar to the Malibu home in need of serious care. Erik found dirt in all plumbing pipes, filled with dirt from kitchen sink, garbage disposal, electrical wiring pulled out and other sabotage from last tenants, to guarantee the sprawling Spanish style ranch house was not rentable or livable. Then, either the last tenants or thieves took many antique fixtures. Erik fixed all. Had a classic corner fireplace, raised hearth, rounded, in living room, opened to enclosed patio. The thick adobe walls kept it cool in the summer.

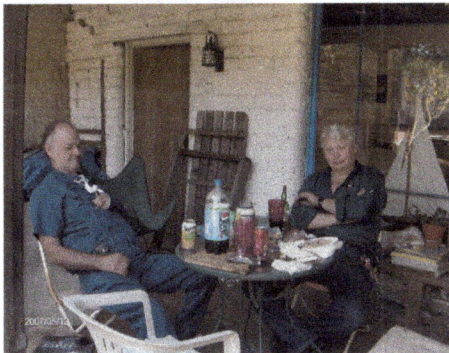

Art and Erik relax on the patio. Erik is home from the hospital.

This was during the Iraq War. Erik was a pacifist. He was known as the Keeper of the La Fayette Crosses. Each service person who died had a La Fayette Cross erected in their name. Erik was in the news again…

Erik sailed the Defiance in protest of the Iraq War.

Erik, Rudy (dog), Mark, and Art Hanson

Around 1991, Laurie and Erik were out for a drink in a standard Malibu haunt. It was crowded, but Erik had secured two seats. He left for the bar and returned with the two drinks. A man was in his seat. Erik said he politely asked the man to move and was refused. Laurie apologized and said she had told the man the seat was taken. Erik said "You heard the lady. Please move." The man sneered, said something like "Make me," and Erik threw one punch to the guy's chin sending him flying up and out of the chair. After the man landed on the floor nearby, Erik sat down. Laurie was pretending to be upset because then they were all thrown out, but she looked happy. I think she was more in awe that he'd apply all that power to keeping her safe.

I was reading Malcolm Gladwell's (c. 2000) The Tipping Point, about how one person can make a difference. The author speaks of certain people who are connectors, more joined to others in the scheme of social fabric and so able to carry messages and materials easier than those more reticent. He mentioned Paul Revere and his social activism vs. Williams Dawes. Revere sounded the alarm and people knew him and came against the British. Dawes sounded a warning which was mostly ignored. From one sizable town only two men came to fight the next day. Dawes was not recognized like Revere. Erik was a connector. The requirement is not that all love him but that many interact with him and know him, recognizing his experience. Prior to the computer, Erik ran up phone bills of several hundred dollars a month sometimes with his connectedness. After computers, I bought him one to get him a chance to email and keep in touch more affordably. He blogged, had a website, sold a licensed product on-line, one of my inventions, and kept regular email contact with friends, acquaintances and researchers around the world.

Chapter Nineteen
Rescuing Erik

Art and I were watching television one night in Los Angeles. We got a call. I recognized Erik's voice. We heard his agitation and his emphasis that I was to remember his computer password. He said he was in a hospital and couldn't get out. He was adamant that I get his things and save his dog and cat. His call was cut off. Art and I looked at each other. "You have to go" "I have to go" we said at the same time. Art couldn't get off work with no notice. He worked for the City of Los Angeles. I called Mother. She'd always liked Erik. We girls had always noticed that if we broke up with a guy, they would always keep coming around to visit with Mom. This was annoying. But, in this instance, it was God's Hand. Mom helped locate Erik and lent the appropriate ballast of respectability to our foray to locate Erik. Mark was 12 at the time. We all scooted up the 5 freeway to La Fayette, California, Erik's last address, a few hundred miles north. He wasn't home. We scoured hospitals. We checked with county welfare. We checked the morgue. We looked everywhere. Art monitored us and gave ideas as he put in a request for vacation time.

Mom and I found a hospital that might have Erik. We went there, with Mark. We were given the once over by nursing staff. I said I was Erik's sister. I introduced Mom as "Mom." The nurse said "Her last name doesn't match. It's Donofrio." Mom went into "theocratic concealment" mode. This means misdirection by not mentioning everything, never(!) lying... She looked innocently at the nurse and kept silent, waiting for me to handle it. Her gray eyes with brown flecks went round and humble. "She remarried." Mom nodded earnestly and kept quiet.

We were told that Erik Beckjord was there. He'd been brought in for admittance to the mental hospital, according to his caretaker. The caretaker had insisted that Erik needed to be locked up. Now, Erik had had several radiation therapy treatments for his pancreatic cancer. It had crumbled his bones. He could not really walk much, very little, actually, with a walker. The nurse said that when they talked to him he seemed lucid and they could find no reason to detain him nor to put him into a mental hospital, which confinement his caretaker kept insisting he needed. The nurse said his brain was fine. She took us to the ward where Erik was. He'd been told we were coming. He was a gentleman to the end. Here he was, in a hospital bed, unable to leave, in hospital "clothes" and he'd had the nurses bring him two fresh water glasses and a fresh jug of water with ice in it. He offered us libations. Even Mom was smart enough to say "Yes, thank-you." We talked to him. He was matter-of-fact. He told how he'd put Chris's name on his bank account to pay the bills for him. He told how she was urging the nurses to put him in a mental ward. We hissed and gnashed our teeth in anger. We got him out. We did not leave without him. We were afraid they would "disappear him" if we left. We felt the pressure of the Holy Spirit Not to Leave Him. We drove home with Erik. Erik reminded my son, Mark, that he'd promised he would take care of Erik's pets. When we, (Art, Mom, Mark, and I) brought Erik home the last time to take care of Erik, we found his communications cut off. To an extrovert living on his own, on a hilltop with no geographical neighborhood nearby, this was very hard to bear. The phone on his desk was absent the cord between the handset and the base. I found the main phone line dead, the internet cut off for an unpaid bill, tv cable cut off for nonpayment. The door to his computer room was locked. Art used to be a locksmith (all the guys in East L.A. claim that they can pick locks because of legitimate reasons). Art got the computer room open, with Erik's nine file cabinets, 45 drawers of files. When I went through his things, I had to thin out to only what we could pack in Art's truck. I culled records and UFO files and Bigfoot and tried to keep the most important stuff. I did all this while knowing I was fighting Erik's system of renaming important things to "family photos" or "Cowboys and Indians." [note: right, Terri? M.] I knew his style, abbreviations, and what he'd told me. He was always fearful of

149

theft, while he was out in the woods or somewhere doing research.

Erik had always supported himself and paid his bills. The medical condition had required him to seek in-house help and he'd had a caretaker on his account to take care of his bills and pay them as needed. I had urged him to take a former married girlfriend, now divorced, who had been repeatedly nagging him to take her as a caretaker. Once again, I butted into someone else's affairs to their sorrow. She wanted some opportunity to torture him. Those five months with a caretaker really messed up his financial affairs. She took his money and didn't pay the bills, even though she was paid by the county to take care of him. We lined up a caretaker nursing service for Erik. I took care of him until we lined up care. Mom cleaned the kitchen and worked through the house. I listed electronics needed and got his computer working after Art picked the locks we needed opened. Erik was a licensed distributor of one of my inventions and I was gratified and impressed to see how many orders had come in while he was locked up. I think he'd been locked up about two weeks before we found him. Erik made some phone calls to close friends to tell them he was "home."

The evidence of how hard it was on Erik to have been in-hospital with no working cell phone or internet was evident when he got home. The first thing he did as the heaviest sedatives wore off was to try to call his cell phone company to see why his phone didn't call out. Erik was thrilled when we got him a new cell phone so he could call. But, when at Brun's House the last week of his life, someone, a homeless man, Alfonso, who Erik used as a groundskeeper and electrical assistant, had given his phone number to the caretaker the police had ordered not to return to his house. He happily answered his phone, per the nurse, only to become extremely agitated as he listened. The nurse reported listening in and hearing cursing and filthy language. They had to sedate Erik after that. We were so sorry that, apparently, he'd been in evil hands for his last days. I was reminded of Mother

Teresa who would remove the dying street people from the filth in which they lived. She took people in to let them die in peace, relative comfort, and dignity. I felt we'd come up to minister to him and help him die in peace. We were grateful to get him into Brun's House the last few days. We'd heard it was rare for anyone to be accepted. They took Erik. We felt it was God's Hand.

On that final trip to Erik's, we saw many things we felt were evidence of God's loving hand on Erik. One example of God's hand was when my mother and I were standing in the driveway and a man came up and said "Who takes care of the bills?"

I held out my hand as I resignedly said "I do." It was a 48-hour (24?) notice of intention to shut off the water, with the amount due written on it: $84.11. While I was yet standing there, my cell phone rang. It was maybe 5 minutes later. The call was from Art, who had left with Erik's dog, Toby. He was calling from our home in Los Angeles, California.

"You'll never believe it! I was home and this man walked up to me and bought some tools and I have $85 pure profit after the cost of the tools." I told him to send it up. After the cost of the money order and stamp it was $85. The Shepherd was bringing His sheep home and easing his comfort.

We realized as I cared for Erik while we waiting for the process to qualify him for homecare and a male caregiver, that he wouldn't walk again, save for a few steps. He was able to enter Bruns House. It is a legend for merciful nursing care and kindness. After the last visit to Erik, when Twinky changed in the twinkling of an eye when we opened the cage to release her to Erik, we knew that the animals knew him for the softy he was. We were all thankful we had rescued Erik. Twinky, the cat, went on to rule our house and torture the dog. She was buried with honors in the yard. Toby, the dog, lived out his days mostly in the patio. He was too big to dig a hole for, so he was cremated and then buried. The birds of Laurie, Cheep and Meep, were housed at Mom's.

I've tried to give a taste of the variety of adventures of Erik and of his steadfast character. He was indeed an Eagle Scout to emulate. Mark went on to become an Eagle Scout "like Uncle Erik" and then to achieve "double silver palms" above that in his troop. They hadn't known of palms before Mark earned six. Erik is honored in our house. He died June 22, 2008. I always appreciated his being a gentleman and dying the day before Art and My anniversary. Erik was a good man, a good friend to Art, a curmudgeon when he wanted to be, but never to me. We sold our minivan; Mark was getting bigger anyway and a jeep let us roust Scouts anywhere in the woods. The money from the van helped get Erik home to the family plot. His sailboat had paid the way to his cremation. Art made him a pine box. We decorated it with carved and burned-in Bigfoot symbols and symbols of the Celtic Christians and Merlin, their archbishop. The symbol of the grail castle, boy scout symbols, and others covered him.

Erik sculled the Great Lakes when he was younger. He was also an Alpine rescue skier in Europe when he lived in Germany. He had a huge old pair of skis. I saw him ski and he was awesome to watch, never faltering, from the top of the lift down. The only skiing I did farther than a bunny hill was with Erik. Happily, I didn't fall.

Duluth

Duluth struck me as amazingly like San Francisco, hills overlooking the big water body. When we buried Erik a huge flock of Canadian geese were flying over. They heard the bagpipes. They landed and stood in straight rows during the service. I took pictures as they started to break up after the service. It was God's Hand. Our small group was joined by the woman in charge of the grounds that day. Erik was laid to rest in his family plot. My friend, an ordained minister, had met us in Chicago and come along. She knew Erik well. The piper he supplied for both of his parents was fitting for his send-off. We had dinner afterward at the famous Duluth restaurant on the Bay at which Erik had attended his High School Prom.

Mark and I read Ecclesiastes 6:3 as a part of our Bible reading that night, as we closed the day after the burial. We didn't plan it. It was the next section. It speaks of the man who "does not even have a proper burial, I say that a stillborn child is better off than he." We rejoiced that Erik had a proper burial, as it obviously was a mark of respect and dignity and God cared about it enough to put it in our reading that night.

Bibliography

Beckjord, J. E. *Frontiers of Science,* Apr(?) *1981*: 105. Print.
Gladwell, Malcolm. The Tipping Point. Hachette Group Pub., 2006. Print.
Isachsen, O. & Berens, L. Working Together, a Personality-Centered Approach to Management 3rd ed. San Juan Capistrano, CA.:Institute for Management Development, 1995 Print
LeFever, Marlene D. Learning Styles, Reaching Everyone God Gave You to Teach. Colorado: David C. Cooke, Pub, 1995. Print.
The Boy Scout Handbook, Eleventh Ed. Irving, Texas: Boy Scouts of America, 1998. Print.
J. E. Beckjord, MBA, and Bruce S. Maccabee, PhD. Report: "Unusual Photographs From Loch Ness," Beckjord, 1988. Print.

Index

Meldrum, PhD, Jeff 3, 79, 102
Mensa 18, 45, 46, 73, 139
Mermaid 23, 118
Mother Teresa 48-49, 150
Mount Elvis 137-138
Munns, Bill 3, 102
Museum 3, 19, 24, 27, 37, 38, 40, 60, 73, 86, 102, 132, 140
Myers-Briggs Inventory 18
National Geographic Society 23, 118
Neon 24
Nicole Brown Simpson 23
Nobel Prize 26, 57
Ogopogo 112, 114, 136
Oregon 71, 72, 78, 88
OSHA 24
Pacific Film Archive 73
Patterson 3, 4, 26-27, 30, 39, 45, 51, 58, 70-71, 75, 85-87, 95-96, 102, 121, 137
People's Park 21, 73
Pongid 74
Puget Sound 58, 83
Ross 59
Rudy 33, 35, 146
Sarich, Vince, of UCB 78, 77, 86
Schaeffer, Robert 4, 26
Scout Law 30, 38, 139
Seckel 26, 28
Si-at-ko, Ski-tuk 66, 73
Skeptics 26-28, 46, 54, 87
Smoke House Road 56, 85
Steiner (Bay Area Skeptics) 26
Stick Indians 77
Thompson, Warren 71
Toby 33, 34, 151
Trancas 27, 38, 140
Tulane, University of 16, 19, 71, 73

Reference Note

[i] He also said that the object is not the kind of thing that is normally found in such lakes: no known fauna from lakes, nor common objects such as logs, algae mats, seaweed, models, submarines, etc., are responsible. I see the object as being reddish-brown to yellow, in different photos. As a personal interpretation, subject to differing opinions, I feel the plume in photo 13 is the same type as in photo no. 15.

Illustrations

Copyright 2017
ISBN: 978-1-7371408-3-2
Squirrel Tracks Press

www.ingramcontent.com/pod-product-compliance
Lightning Source LLC
Chambersburg PA
CBHW062058270326
41931CB00013B/3129